The Judge and the Umpire

David H. Moskowitz

www.thecreativepositivist.com

First published by Huge Jam, Bedford, 2022

ISBN: 978-1-7391829-1-5

To Marian

Other books in this series:

The Judge and the Philosopher
The Judge and the President
The Judge and the Incorrect Decision

ACKNOWLEDGMENTS

In writing this book, I have received assistance from many people, and I want to thank especially the following persons for their help. Three law students from Villanova Law School, Justin Kramer, Laura Phyz and Michelle E. Strauck, performed valuable research. Camden Delphus also assisted with research. The following individuals read the first draft of the book and offered comments—Mindy Brook, Ruth Schultz, Robert Romain, Nathaniel Smith, Leo Zamparelli, Helman Brook, Phil Frost, Ron Stengel and Ken Mumma. Michelle Dempsey, a professor at Villanova Law School, who also received a D.Phil. from Oxford University, has also been very helpful. Mindy Brook, Ruth Schultz and Marian Moskowitz read the second draft of this book and provided comments and insight that improved the book immensely. Mary Lawrence has edited the endnotes. Jacqueline Tobin has served as my professional editor, agent and publisher.

I would not have been able to write this book (or, truth be told, accomplish whatever I have achieved) without the active support, encouragement and problem-solving of my wife, Marian Moskowitz. Finally, I cannot find the words to explain how much I enjoyed and benefitted from my two years of weekly sessions with H.L.A. Hart, and I am eternally grateful to him for his willingness to guide me in my studies and to teach me about many subjects, including, of course, jurisprudence. While Hart is no longer with us, he remains the standard bearer for the revitalization of legal philosophy and the modern version of legal positivism.

DHM, October 2022

CONTENTS

Introduction

This book is the direct result of the time I spent studying at Oxford University during 1960 to 1963 and the indirect result of an event that occurred in 2018. In 2018, Judge Brett Kavanaugh was nominated for appointment to the U.S. Supreme Court. He testified in his confirmation hearing before the U.S. Senate Judiciary Committee that the role of a judge (including a justice of the Supreme Court) was similar to the role of an umpire in a baseball game. This appeared to me to be a questionable statement. My immediate thought was that I should attempt to clarify it based upon my experience and knowledge about what I thought a judge actually does and how we should evaluate what he does.

The events in the 1960s that led to writing this book were more significant. I graduated from college with a degree in accounting (Penn State, 1957). I finished law school three years later (Villanova Law School, 1960). Before I started practicing law, I decided that I should obtain an education in many subjects, including history, literature, economics, sociology, psychology, politics and philosophy.

I was admitted to Wadham College in Oxford University, and I arrived there in September 1960. I attended lectures and started reading books in the subjects I just mentioned. The law tutor in

Wadham College, Mr. P.B. Carter, called me to his office and informed me that I needed to work under the supervision of a tutor. He offered to tutor me in law. My goal, however, was not to study law. I decided to seek a tutor.

I was attending the lectures of Professor H.L.A. Hart, who was the Professor of Jurisprudence. I approached him after a lecture and asked him if he would be my tutor. We discussed the subjects that I wanted to study, and he agreed to tutor me. I met with him once a week for the 1960-61 academic year and we talked about many subjects. Each week he would name six to ten books that I should read before the next session. The books that I did not finish during the week were left for the breaks between the trimesters.

We went from subject to subject. Even though we often did not finish the prior week's discussion, we frequently started a new topic and went off into tangents involving other issues and additional authors whose books Hart thought I should read. We talked about the lectures that I was attending, and he recommended other lectures that I should also attend (Roman law, philosophy of the mind, all lectures given by Isaiah Berlin, Cecil Roth's seminars, for some examples). Hart seemed to be knowledgeable about all subjects and he introduced me to many authors and a treasure chest of concepts, issues, ideas and theories.

The year with Hart was the most productive year of my life. I felt that I was learning so much and I became aware of so much that I did not know that I decided that I wanted to continue working with Hart for a second year. I asked him if he would tutor me for another year. Hart explained to me that he generally did not tutor undergraduate students, that he no longer remembered why he had agreed to tutor me for the year we had just finished, and that, while he thought that I had exhibited great growth during the year and had worked very hard, he wanted to concentrate on supervising graduate students.

I asked Hart if I could become a graduate student. He hesitated and I requested that he give me a test to see if I would qualify. Hart did not immediately answer, and I waited for a response. He then said that he had just finished writing a book and my test would be my critique of the book when I returned after the summer break. He gave me the galley proofs for *The Concept of Law*.

I returned in September 1961 and met with Hart. As I recall, the discussion started at approximately ten o'clock in the morning and continued into the evening. I told Hart that the book was beautifully written, so well written that it seduced the reader into accepting the legal philosophy that the book described. I told him that the book would be a classic (though I did not appreciate then how much of a classic it would be—ultimately it became the most important book written in legal philosophy in the 20th century). I then proceeded with my criticism of the book.

While we discussed many of the ideas that were presented in the book, my primary focus was on what judges did in making judicial decisions. I did not agree with Hart's view of judicial discretion. I did not think that judges made judicial decisions by simply applying existing law. I thought then, and I still believe, that there are other factors besides the law that are involved in the making of judicial decisions. At the end of this marathon session, Hart said that he thought that my critique of his book included some important points that we should continue discussing during the school year and he declared that I was now a graduate student and that I should write a thesis for the D.Phil. degree.

We met for a second year, continuing some of the discussions left over from the prior year, touching upon many of the issues in *The Concept of Law* and developing the ideas that became part of my doctoral thesis. I finished the thesis after the second year with Hart and I received the D.Phil. degree after the oral defense of my thesis in April 1963.

This book and the other three books that I will mention below contain the ideas that were included in my doctoral thesis. I have wanted to write these books for many years. Since my two years at Oxford, I have been a judicial clerk for several judges, practiced law for close to 50 years, taught in college and law school and participated in multiple entrepreneurial ventures.

In 2018, I listened to Judge Kavanaugh's description of the role of a judge, and I decided that it was time for me to write these books. This book, *The Judge and the Umpire*, includes six cases which I have selected to illustrate that a judge when making a judicial decision may not only apply existing law but may also refer to alternate sources. In other words, judges sometimes change the existing law and create new law when they make their decisions.

Umpires, like judges, strive to make correct decisions. But judges may also make decisions that would not qualify as correct legal decisions because they consider other factors besides the existing legal rules. Umpires apply only the existing rules of baseball.

The theory that judges consider alternate sources and that those who study judicial decisions should consider these alternate sources in evaluating and criticizing judicial decisions bears some similarity to legal theories presented by other legal philosophers. To point out this consistency and to contrast the legal theory that I am presenting, which I call "creative positivism," with other legal philosophies, I have written a second book entitled *The Judge and the Philosopher*. In *The Judge and the Philosopher*, I discuss Hart's legal theories and the legal theories of some other legal philosophers. I discuss in detail Hart's theory of judicial discretion, which is my primary departure from Hart's legal philosophy.

In my third book, which I call *The Judge and the President*, I expand Hart's rule of recognition by considering various situations which do not fit neatly into the rule of recognition. I also introduce the role of customary rules, the concept of the real rules (law in action or the actual rules that are administered), and other types of rules that are not usually considered in legal positivism (which is the jurisprudential theory that Hart revived, which has become the prominent legal theory in the past sixty years).

In the fourth book, *The Judge and the Incorrect Decision*, I supplement Hart's version of legal positivism and his legal system of primary and secondary rules with a third class of rules which I call "tertiary rules." The tertiary rules include the three elements of the judicial decision (the correct decision, the just decision and the wise decision, which are described in this book), Finally, I describe in detail the legal philosophy of creative positivism.

My goal is to have the four books complement each other, with this book presenting actual cases that support the ideas incorporated into creative positivism and the second book concentrating on other legal philosophies and how they lead to creative positivism. The third book supplements Hart's legal philosophy and the fourth book describes creative positivism. My goal is to defend and support my legal theory by referring to six actual cases as examples of the correct decision the just decision and the wise decision. I hope this book will be of interest to the average reader, including those persons who may not be interested in jurisprudence. Volumes 2-4 are more technical and assume some knowledge about law and legal systems.

Creative positivism provides an evaluative vocabulary and methodology for studying, analyzing and discussing judicial decisions. It may also provide insight into how judicial decisions are reached. It can be viewed as a framework for displaying the historical, moral, social and political factors that are the fundamental values supporting the making of judicial decisions and the creation of new legal rules.

The first chapter in this book compares the role of judges to that of umpires. Chapter Two presents a case decided by a trial court involving the enforceability of a contract between an employer and an employee. The employee terminated his employment and wanted to compete with his former employer by contacting the employer's customers. Dealing with the employer's customers was prohibited by the contract the employee had signed. In this case, the judge applied the existing law, making a correct decision, but he was obviously troubled by his decision because he questioned whether the decision was moral and ethical. I attempt in the third chapter to define the correct decision.

In the fourth chapter, I present a case involving a company that was accused of environmental pollution. The company claimed that it had insurance coverage for the costs involved in remediating the pollution (the clean-up costs). The insurance company insisted that the events creating the pollution did not satisfy the standard in the insurance policy of a "sudden and accidental" event so that the insurance company was not obligated to pay for the cost of rectifying the pollution.

I characterize the decision by an intermediate appellate court n this case in Chapter Four as an incorrect decision. I distinguish the incorrect decision that is the result of a mistake from the decision intentionally to not make a correct decision (in other words, the decision intentionally to create a new legal rule and not to apply the existing law, so that this decision will not be consistent with the law that existed before the decision was made).

The third case that I consider, in Chapter Five, involved a worker in a mill injuring himself in order to protect another worker from being killed or injured. The worker whose life was saved promised to make biweekly payments to the disabled worker for the lifetime of the disabled worker. While pursuant to the law that existed when this case was decided, the promise to make the payments was not legally enforceable, the court decided to create a new legal rule and to hold that the promise constituted a legally binding contract. The court made what I would contend is a just decision.

Similar to judges sometimes attempting to make just decisions, judges may also sometimes change the law in order to make wise decisions. These wise decisions may modify the law as a result of consideration of the effects of the decision as a precedent (in other words, consideration of the consequences of the decision being made upon the society and the making of future decisions).

My illustration of the wise decision in Chapter Six is a case in which the U.S. Supreme Court decided to overturn an almost one-hundred-year-old precedent in order to require federal courts to refrain from applying federal law and apply, instead, the law of the state that was relevant to the event being considered. This case involved an individual who was injured in Pennsylvania when he was struck by a door on a railroad car and Pennsylvania law was applied rather than federal law.

I then consider two other cases in which the courts made unjust, wise decisions. In Chapter Seven, the dispute was between the builder of a house and the purchaser of the house who was complaining about construction defects. The trial court found in favor of the builder, the intermediate appellate court reversed the trial court and decided that the homeowner should prevail, and the Supreme Court of Pennsylvania reversed the intermediate appellate court and decided to reinstate the decision of the trial court. I conclude that this was a correct, unjust and wise decision.

In Chapter Eight, I discuss a case that I would maintain is an incorrect, unjust and wise decision. It involves the trustee of a bankrupt company (it was a trust fund) being obligated to reimburse the company for losses suffered by the company as a result of the disloyalty of two employees retained by the trustee to continue managing the company. Prior to this decision, no trustee had ever been found to be personally liable for the fraudulent acts of his employees when he himself received no personal benefit resulting from their fraudulent practices.

In Chapter Nine, I revisit the six cases by applying the three elements to evaluate them. These three elements of the judicial decision—correctness, justice and wisdom—are the foundation for creative positivism, which I briefly introduce in Chapter Ten. Chapter Eleven is a short summary of why I have concluded that judges are not like umpires.

While this book is not primarily about my personal experiences, I have included three appendices that relate to the cases and to my experiences as a legal practitioner. Appendix A is a memorandum of an interview that I had with the judge who decided the first case, which is the case of the employee who wanted to compete with his former employer. Appendix B is about my experience as a law clerk to a trial judge. Appendix C concerns my use of legal philosophy in representing clients in various jurisdictions.

I.
Judges Are Not Umpires

Justices for the U.S. Supreme Court are nominated by the President and must be approved by the Senate. Senatorial confirmation hearings for Supreme Court nominees are political theatre (think of the American version of Gilbert and Sullivan's *Trial by Jury*). During these hearings, candidates for Supreme Court judgeships compare the role of a judge, particularly one who will potentially receive a lifetime appointment to the highest court in the land, to an umpire calling balls and strikes in a baseball game. This is a supreme mischaracterization of what a judge does.

1.1 Chief Justice John G. Roberts, Jr.
Chief Justice John G. Roberts, Jr., in his Senatorial confirmation hearing, began his introductory remarks by describing his view about exercising judicial powers: "Judges are like umpires. Umpires don't make the rules; they apply them. The role of an umpire and a judge is critical. They make sure everybody plays by the rules. But it is a limited role."[1]

1.2 Justice Brett M. Kavanaugh
Justice Brett M. Kavanaugh, at his Senatorial confirmation hearing,

referred to Chief Justice Roberts' statement as a great description of the role of judges. Justice Kavanaugh said that: "A good judge must be an umpire—a neutral and impartial arbiter who favors no litigant or policy."[2] He also gave a one-hour lecture at Catholic University's Columbus School of Law on April 1, 2015, about the role of judges being comparable to the role of umpires.[3]

Chief Justice Roberts and Justice Kavanaugh, therefore, equated the function of a judge (they both were judges on the Court of Appeals at the time of their nomination to the Supreme Court) as comparable to the role of an umpire in a baseball game. Chief Justice Roberts, in an effort to establish that he would decide cases in accordance with pre-existing law (that is, law that was law before he made his decision) and would avoid making decisions based upon his personal politics (or anything other than the pre-existing law), insisted that he would decide cases according to the rule of law. More specifically, he said that a judge was like an umpire calling balls and strikes in a baseball game.[4]

1.3 The umpire and the judge

Umpires in baseball and judges in the judicial system are both decision makers. They wear distinctive clothing to differentiate them from other participants in the activities in which they are involved.[5] They both apply rules in making their decisions. In doing so, they each have limited areas of discretion and are required to interpret the applicable rules. Therefore, there are some similarities in their performance of their respective jobs.

Baseball, like the law, has its own language, unique to the activity with which umpires are involved. Suppose that someone unfamiliar with baseball but fluent in the English language hears the radio announcer of a baseball game state that the batter has three balls and one strike. He might wonder why the batter was out on strike (assuming that the reference was to a labor dispute rather than to one player striking another player) and why he needed three balls. Unless he learns the way in which words are used in baseball, he will be unable to understand the game.

The same observation is even more true of the law. Our observer would also have a difficult time understanding what an assault and battery is. If he knew that an assault was a criminal offense, he might still think that a battery is an apparatus that is used to store electrical energy. The vocabulary of the law frequently borrows terms from other languages and employs concepts and metaphors that often appear to be quite obscure and difficult to comprehend.

Some of the terms used in baseball and in the law, even if they appear to be clear, and even if they are very clear in ordinary language, may have acquired a very different meaning in baseball and in the law. Both the judge and the umpire must use specialized language when they apply their respective sets of rules.

Language in both baseball and law can often be unclear, ambiguous and vague. Baseball rules, however, are more specific than legal rules. Moreover, legal rules are about many more varied forms of human behavior than baseball, so they are more complex than baseball rules and lend themselves to a greater degree of interpretation. Baseball rules are contained in one book, while legal rules may be found in a law library that can be the size of a house.

In Chapter Four, we will consider a case involving whether the creating of environmental pollution over many years would qualify as "sudden and accidental." It took two sessions in the trial court and two appearances before the Court of Appeals to resolve the matter. The reader will be able to decide whether he thinks the decisions were correct and whether the ends of justice were served in the resolution of this dispute. Your conclusion about this case will be somewhat dependent upon two other cases decided by the Indiana Supreme Court. Therefore, multiple lengthy and detailed opinions in six different decisions are relevant to your assessment of whether you agree with the result. This is far different from whether you agree that a pitch in a baseball game is a ball or a strike.

In addition, whether it is the judge or the umpire, the exercise of decision-making authority is context specific. They act in the context of a system that not only includes the use of specialized language that is a necessary feature of their decision-making processes but is also subject to customary rules about the decision-making process. Umpires are supposed to treat the two teams equally, using the same strike zone for both teams. Judges have the responsibility to ensure fair trials.

Baseball has a commissioner and a legislative body that makes the rules. Decision-making in baseball in some respects does resemble decision-making in a legal system, though the legal system has a much more elaborate hierarchy. There are trial courts, intermediate appellate courts and supreme courts. Multiple forms of legislatures and other agencies and officials make the laws, and, in some systems, the judiciary, in addition to itself being empowered to make laws, has the authority to exercise checks and balances on the executive and legislative branches of the government.

In a modern democratic society, there is an institutionalized system providing for a hierarchy of courts. There is an established methodology for appealing to a higher court to review the activities of lower courts. There is a formal elaborate set of appellate rules, some written and some unwritten, in the legal system. Review of the decisions of umpires is rare and changing a call from a ball to a strike virtually never happens.

In the judicial hierarchy, the superior courts influence (control, dictate) the decisions of the trial courts which try to avoid being reversed by the appellate courts.[6] The type of lawsuit may also be a factor in how the judge approaches the case. Some cases will involve significant public issues, and some will not. In *The Judge and the President*, we consider lawsuits involving presidential elections.

In baseball, umpiring in a playoff game may appear to be different than umpiring an ordinary game. One might expect there is a difference between the 3-2 count to the first batter and the 3-2 pitch in the 9th inning with the bases loaded and the score tied, though the strike zone remains the same. Mitchell N. Berman, a professor of law and philosophy at the University of Pennsylvania Law School, concludes, however, that "temporal variance" rarely occurs in baseball. He contends that the strike zone does not change at the end of games. Temporal variance, however, according to Berman, can be observed in football and basketball games (the rules do not change, but the application of the rules is relaxed at the end of close games, so that the official lets the result be determined by the athletes and not by the officials).[7]

Judges, in contrast to umpires, do exhibit temporal variance and do make decisions that reflect many factors. Some cases are vastly more important than other cases and are much more important than a baseball game. I will discuss many cases in this book and the different types of cases and situations presented to judges are very variable, as will become obvious.

1.4 The rules of baseball

So, what is an umpire doing when he calls balls and strikes? Let's look at the Official Rules of Baseball.[8] Section 200 has the definitions of the terms used in the Official Rules. A "ball" is defined as follows: "A BALL is a pitch which does not enter the strike zone in flight and is not struck at by the batter." To understand this definition, we must know the definitions of the following additional terms: "in flight," "pitch," "strike zone," "struck at," and "batter." "In flight" is defined, for example, as a ball that has not touched the ground.

Consider now the term "strike zone" to understand what "a ball" is. This is the area above home base (which is also a defined term and is sometimes referred to as "home plate") that is between the hollow beneath the kneecap and midway between the top of the batter's pants and the top of his shoulders (more or less, the strike zone, then, is between the batter's knees and the letters on his uniform). This strike zone is not visibly depicted and is something of an abstraction. You cannot see it. You must imagine it is there. You must judge whether the ball passes through this imaginary strike zone.

In umpiring and judging, there may be clear situations and there may be close calls. The umpire and the judge must make a decision in all situations that are presented to them, and it is often an either-or decision. The pitch is either a ball or a strike. It is never too close to call. It is not a question of degree (it is similar to "you can't be slightly pregnant"). The pitch cannot be replayed (even instant replay is just the umpire checking his own call). Judgment by the umpire is clearly required.

Moreover, the umpire like the judge should not be arbitrary. He should apply the rules consistently in making his decisions. While the lawyers on both sides of a case may cite contradictory authorities to the judge, the judge must decide what the correct decision will be. This does not mean that everyone will agree about which decision would be the correct decision. It does not mean that there will not be hard cases.

Chief Justice Roberts is right when he observes that, like the umpire calling the close pitch a ball or a strike, the judge must decide the case that is presented to him. He also insists that he would be a modest judge, that is, a judge who does not make legislative decisions but simply applies the law correctly. Chief Justice Robert's testimony is not unusual. Robert Bork was candid in his answers to questions about how he would decide cases and he was not confirmed by the Senate. Since then, all the nominees for judicial appointments claim to decide cases generally in accordance with pre-existing law and to avoid deciding cases in accordance with their own personal biases.[9]

1.5 A decision may be correct or incorrect

It is possible that both the judge and the umpire may make an incorrect decision. The umpire may call a pitch a strike that is outside the strike zone. The judge may err in finding and interpreting the applicable legal rule. Each of them may make an incorrect decision, which is incorrect as the result of making a mistake. In the case that I mentioned involving environmental pollution, the judges made a mistake about what rule of law should be applied to decide the case before them.

The judge and the umpire may also make a correct decision. Arriving at the correct decision is a reasoning process, and it need not be an evaluative process. Evaluative reasoning is possible and useful only if there is a willingness and a capability of reaching an alternative decision. As I will explain in Chapter Three, evaluation is not necessary if you are only interested in the correct decision. Umpires are obligated to make the correct decision. They have no obligation to evaluate their decision. Justice has no place in their decision. There is no just result in a baseball game, and, similarly, justice is not involved in whether a pitch is a ball or a strike.

The incorrect decision for the umpire is always a mistake. The umpire always wants to make the correct decision. The judge may want to make a decision that does not qualify as the correct decision and she has the authority to make a decision that is not consistent with the pre-existing law (and is, therefore, an incorrect decision).

Umpires make the correct decision and do not consider whether it is a just decision. Judges also have the obligation to make the correct decision, but they also have the power and the authority to make the just decision. In Chapter Five, we will consider a case in which the judge looked to justice in making his decision. In Chapters Six to Eight, the judges considered the consequences of their decisions. The correct decision may not always be the best decision.

1.6 The alternate source decision

I will argue that the judge, unlike the umpire, may also reach an "alternate source decision." I will explain this in the chapters that follow. For a shorthand description, it is not a decision made as a result of an error in applying the legal rules but is an intentional decision which the judge knows, or should know, is inconsistent with the pre-existing law. It is an incorrect decision, but it is not the result of the judge making a mistake.

If Chief Justice Roberts and Justice Kavanaugh are right that they acting as judges would only call balls and strikes, they would never change the law. But the law will often change as a result of judicial decisions. They have not acknowledged that published judicial decisions often change the law and that they as judges can make alternate source decisions with the necessary result that they will be involved in changing the law. In fact, judges frequently make new law.[10]

Neither an umpire, nor a referee, nor a judge at a dog show has the authority to change the rules. A judge deciding a legal case, especially at an appellate level, not only has the authority to change the rules but she often cannot avoid doing so. While a judge is not a legislator, deciding cases may involve changing the law, and claiming that a judge just follows the law is a misrepresentation.[11]

Umpires cannot change the rules and judges cannot avoid changing the rules. Judges, in fact, have the authority to engage in law creation and do so. This is a major difference in the role of a judge in comparison to that of an umpire. Equating judging legal cases to calling balls and strikes is highly misleading.

Courts of law are ultimately courts of justice. In a modern democratic society with the rule of law, we expect judges to decide cases as independent arbiters and not to be bound by outdated rules that could provide for absurd results in an individual case. Courts must act as an independent branch of government, and, to ensure they do so, Supreme Court Justices and other federal judges are appointed for life.

For Chief Justice Roberts and Justice Kavanaugh to claim, then, that they will not act like judges in a modern, democratic legal system, but that they will mechanically apply pre-existing law and decide cases in accordance with some objective standard of a legal strike zone, is not accurate. This is not to suggest that judges decide cases by whim or bias or fail to apply a rational reasoning process to decide cases. Judges try to avoid the effects of their individual biases and do not generally substitute their own views for the established public policies and underlying legal principles that are part of the legal system. Sometimes, however, judges must recognize that the decision in strict application of the pre-existing law may not be the best decision.

1.7 Rules of games

Comparing legal rules with rules of games has been prevalent in jurisprudential studies for many years, especially by English authors.[12] Alf Ross, a Scandinavian legal realist, in *On Law and Justice*, uses the example of an observer watching a game of chess in order to illustrate the failure to notice that the rules of games are significantly different from legal rules.[13] Comparing legal rules with the rules of chess can be somewhat misleading.

When an opponent moves the bishop to the right horizontally in a straight line rather than diagonally, we merely remind him of the relevant rule, unless we think that he is trying to cheat. We expect that a reminder will be sufficient. The remedy for the illegal move is for the opponent to declare that it is illegal and to require that a legal move be substituted for the illegal move. In other words, this statement will, in ordinary circumstances, elicit a new move in conformity with the rules. If our opponent refuses to move his bishop in accordance with the rules of the game, either there is a discontinuance of the game because of this failure to agree upon the rules or there is an explicit or implicit change in the rules. The reaction to a breach of a legal rule is entirely different.

Legal rules presuppose the possibility of their being disobeyed and the chance that the rule will be disobeyed, and the attached sanction applied, is always an accepted possibility (this type of rule is referred to as a duty-imposing rule—the rule prohibits certain conduct, such as committing a crime). A similar concept is also true of power-conferring rules (the rule provides the opportunity to obtain a legal benefit, such as getting married, writing a will or a contract) where there is no sanction attached to failure to observe the rule. Instead, there is a choice of whether to comply with the rule or not, and the cost of non-compliance is the failure to achieve the desired legal result. The difference between a rule of chess which must be complied with for the game to continue in accordance with its rules and these two types of legal rules (the duty-imposing and the power-conferring rules) is obvious.

H.L.A. Hart, who was the professor of jurisprudence at Oxford University when I was a student there, is generally credited with making the distinction between duty-imposing rules and power-conferring rules. He notes this difficulty with the comparison of legal rules to the rules of chess, and he offers an alternative comparison:

"We are able to distinguish a normal game from the game of 'scorer's discretion' simply because the scoring rule, though it has, like other rules, this area of open texture where the scorer has to exercise a choice yet has a core of settled meaning. It is this which the scorer is not free to depart from, and which, so far as it goes, constitutes the standard of correct and incorrect scoring, both for the player, in making his official [sic.] statements as to the score, and for the scorer in his official rulings. It is this that makes it true to say, that the scorer's rulings are, though final, not infallible. The same is true in law."[14]

This comparison, however, is somewhat misleading.

A minor objection to this comparison is that rules of games are usually much clearer and more definite than legal rules. In fact, it is difficult to imagine a game being played with serious disagreement about its rules. Carl A. Auerbach, who was the Dean of the University of Minnesota Law School, mentions a more fundamental objection.

He criticizes the comparison for the reason that one may choose whether he will play a game, but he has no choice whether the law will apply to his activities.[15] It may be added that his decision to play the game may be based upon his implicit acceptance of its rules, and, if he does not agree with the rules, the rules can be modified prior to the commencement of the game and his version of the game played or an acceptable variation of it. This may be the crux of the difference between the rules of games, which are accepted by the participants, and legal rules, which, while applicable, may not be accepted and may even be intentionally disobeyed.

Rules govern how the game is played and the players do not just obey the rules, but they also use the rules in order to play the game. They criticize those who do not follow the rules. Once the game commences, the problems facing the officials are almost solely those of finding and applying the applicable rules.[16] But, in the case of judges, even after the applicable rule is determined, it is still possible for the judge to modify the rule in order to decide the case.

To put this objection a bit differently, it is always possible to argue in a court of law that the pre-existing law (the law prior to the case being decided) should not be applied to this case. To do so, the advocate may not be arguing that the pre-existing law contains a mistake. He is arguing that the pre-existing law should be modified, or an exception created, or it should be extended to cover a new situation. This argument may be based upon the undesirable social effects of the decision if the pre-existing law is applied or the injustice of its application to this case. The argument may be buttressed by an appeal to the desirability of using a legal device to achieve the result, for example, by limiting the decision which established the rule "to its facts," or even overruling the prior decision (I discuss overruling of a prior decision, a precedent, in Section 7.5).

In Chapter Six, I will discuss at some length the *Erie Railroad Co. v. Tompkins* case as a prime example of a decision in which the well-established pre-existing legal rule was not applied and, in fact, the leading precedent was overruled in order to make a major and substantial change in the law. I will argue that the *Erie* case was not a hard case in the sense that the pre-existing law was unclear or ambiguous. I maintain that the applicable legal rule had been settled law for almost 100 years before this decision was made.

The point is that judges are empowered in both England and America to change the pre-existing law. Surely, no official in a game is so empowered, and, in fact, were he, it would be the game that Hart calls "scorer's discretion." I am not suggesting, however, that judges have the authority to change the legal rules in a manner comparable to Hart's version of "scorer's discretion."

The comparison of the role of judges to the role of officials applying the rules of a game is a return to an outdated theory of law, which I call the traditional theory. The judge's function is not simply the finding of the legal rules and applying them to factual situations. The traditional theory does not account for the law's growth and its changeability to meet constantly fresh demands. It is important to note that the pre-existing law is not only augmented but it is also modified. No United States court has denied itself the power to overrule its own precedents.[17] It is this power to change the existing rules that is not granted to officials of a game.

In this book, I will discuss actual cases to support my claim that a typical judge does much more than simply apply the rules and operate like an umpire calling balls and strikes. Both umpires and judges strive to reach correct decisions, but the judge has the authority to change the law in order to make the best decision. Before we get to the cases, I want to clarify some basic concepts about the law.

1.8 Law, legal systems, legal rules and law-actors

Every game has three elements: (1) an organizational structure; (2) a set of rules; and (3) participants (players and, possibly, officials like umpires). The same is true of the law. If there is law, there is a legal system and, in the United States with its federal structure, there are multiple legal systems. There are rules, and I already mentioned duty-imposing rules and power-conferring rules. But there are also other types of rules. Finally, there are participants, and this would include both those officials who make and administer the law and those persons who will be subject to the law (I will call both "law-actors"). I want to introduce these concepts before we consider the cases.

To begin the discussion of the legal system in the U.S., one must start with acknowledging that there is a federal judicial system and 50 individual state judicial systems. The federal system has district courts, which are the basic trial courts. The courts of appeal are the intermediate appellate courts. They do not conduct trials; they decide appeals from the district courts. Within each circuit of the courts of appeals, there may be multiple district courts. There are 94 district courts and 13 courts of appeals. Appeals from the courts of appeals are filed in the Supreme Court, which is the highest court in the land.

This federal system of courts is a hierarchical system. The precedents (the prior legally binding decisions) of the Supreme Court are binding on all the courts below it. The precedents of the court of appeals are binding on all the district courts in their circuit. The decisions in one district court are not binding on the other districts, just as the decision in one court of appeals is not binding on the other courts of appeals. The concept of which decisions are binding, and which are not, is primarily controlled by customary rules. Some decisions that are regarded as non-binding may be cited as an alternate source on the grounds that they are persuasive even though they are non-binding. Therefore, the federal system is a multitude of legal systems in the sense that the pre-existing law in each judicial district is distinct for that district.

Each of the fifty states has its own legal system. Each state has its own hierarchy of trial courts and appellate courts and its own set of customary rules as to which prior decisions are precedential in nature. In fact, in all these judicial systems, there may be decisions that are non-precedential. Many of the state legal systems have trial courts that are organized within individual counties. These county courts are the courts of original jurisdiction. There are more than 3,000 counties in the U.S. Just as one may regard each of the district courts in the federal system as representative of a separate legal system, each of the county legal systems could be viewed as a distinct legal system. There is a hierarchical organization of courts in each state, like that of the federal system. Also, in both the state systems and the federal system, there are different types of courts, such as, for example, juvenile courts or bankruptcy courts.

Each legal system has its own set of legal rules. Legal rules may be created by legislatures by enactment of statutes, by courts by establishing precedents and by the executive branch of the government by executive orders. Legal rules may also be created by administrative agencies in both the federal and the state legal system. Each legal system has its own procedural rules (though there is uniformity in much of the federal legal system and in individual state legal systems) and, in fact, individual trial judges may have their own rules for how trials are conducted in their courtroom.

To make this more confusing, as we will see in Chapter Six, the applicable rules (the rules that will be applied to decide the case) may be the rules of a different jurisdiction than the one in which the case is being tried. For example, the federal courts in a case between citizens of two different states (a diversity-of-citizenship case) will apply the legal rules of the relevant state and not federal common law. Similarly, the courts in one state may apply the law of another state, such as the law of the state in which an automobile accident occurred or in which the property is in a real property case (for example, a case involving the ownership of land).

There are two other conceptual types of legal rules that we will consider. Much of the systematic and institutional nature of legal systems is held together by customary structural and procedural rules. There may also be self-executing substantive customary rules, which are rules established by customs that create legally applicable norms (customs with the force of law). Customary rules are self-enforced, unless they are also customary legal rules that may be legally enforced.

Just as games have players and sometimes have officials, legal systems have subjects and officials. Officials, however, are also subject to the law. Subjects may also establish their own rules that guide their affairs, and these rules may also be in some situations legally enforced. Several of the cases we will consider involve contracts and a contract sets in motion rules that the contracting parties have created themselves to govern their legal relationship. An example of a power-conferring rule is the rule providing for the contract of marriage and the couple getting married may also enter their own individual contract, which is called a pre-nuptial agreement.

The discussion in this section is intended to be introductory and much of what has been stated will be further explained and extended as we consider the cases. I will suggest that there are three elements that should be utilized in the study and evaluation of judicial decisions. Applying the pre-existing law will lead to a correct decision (Chapter Two and Chapter Three). If a mistake is made, it could lead to an incorrect decision (Chapter Four). The judge may also reach a just decision (Chapter Five). My third element is the wise decision (Chapter Six). Both the just decision and the wise decision may be alternate source decisions.[18] I call this theory creative positivism.

To avoid over-emphasis on the United States Supreme Court, I will discuss cases from trial courts and intermediate appellate courts, as well as those from the Supreme Court. Let's start with a trial court decision that is a correct decision.

2.
The Correct Decision

2.1 Factual situation in the *O'Brien* case

Michael O'Brien needed a job. He had attended college for several years and had held a variety of jobs, but he was not satisfied with either the type of work he was doing or the compensation he was receiving. O'Brien's high-school classmate, Blaise DeSanto, Jr., worked for Desco Steel Corp., a company owned by his father, Blaise DeSanto, Sr.

DeSanto, Sr. had started selling steel in 1971 and formed Desco in 1991. The business of Desco was the purchase of rebar and other steel products in bulk and the reselling of these products by "truckload."

The vision of DeSanto, Sr. for Desco was that it would be a family business and he did not generally hire non-family employees. Nonetheless, DeSanto, Sr. had hired two salesmen, Michael Vetter and Barry Benson, who were not family members. They had each previously employed DeSanto, Sr.

O'Brien decided to talk to DeSanto, Jr. to see if he could work at Desco and "learn the business." O'Brien had no experience in the steel and rebar brokerage industry. DeSanto, Sr. knew O'Brien because of his friendship with DeSanto, Jr. during high school. DeSanto, Sr.

regarded O'Brien as part of his family. Therefore, in 2001, DeSanto, Sr. hired O'Brien, who became Desco's third salesman.

Desco's customers were primarily individuals or companies in the construction trade, such as concrete contractors. DeSanto, Sr. had built the business of Desco by "cold calling" suppliers and potential customers. Desco had 300 to 500 active customers. All employees, including O'Brien, had full access to Desco's customer lists, supplier lists, pricing and other important information. O'Brien's job was to locate prospective suppliers and customers, which he did by looking at SuperPages.com, networking with current suppliers and customers, cold calling and other sales techniques. Desco's employees taught O'Brien how to find potential customers, how to bid when purchasing steel and how to price a potential order from a customer.

Between 2001 and 2008, O'Brien developed several new suppliers and more than 100 new customers. Tampa International was his single largest customer, accounting for approximately fifty percent of his income. O'Brien's compensation, like that of the other salesmen, was thirty-five percent of the profit on each sale. O'Brien's commissions in 2006 were $177,000 and his 2007 commissions were $230,725.

In early 2007, Barry Benson, one of the three non-family-member Desco salesmen, left Desco and joined a competitor. DeSanto, Sr. decided that he should request that his two other salesmen sign a non-disclosure and non-competition agreement. DeSanto, Sr. had his attorney prepare the agreement, which he presented to the two remaining salesmen on February 13, 2007. Michael Vetter, the other salesman besides O'Brien, signed the agreement immediately. Michael O'Brien also signed the agreement, though the circumstances of his doing so were in dispute at the trial.

In 2008, Desco withdrew Tampa International's line of credit based on information that DeSanto, Sr. had received from an insurance company in the business of insuring accounts receivable. DeSanto, Sr. told O'Brien why he denied credit to Tampa International. O'Brien was upset with this decision. O'Brien resigned from Desco in November 2008.

O'Brien found it difficult to obtain a job with prospective employers in the steel brokerage industry because he had signed the non-compete agreement. So, he started his own business. He was limited in the amount of bulk steel he could purchase because of credit requirements.

DeSanto, Sr. agreed that O'Brien, notwithstanding the non-compete agreement, could solicit business from the customers he had developed while he was an employee of Desco. O'Brien, however, wanted to solicit business from all Desco's customers. When O'Brien left Desco, he took the customer list without informing Desco that he was doing so. DeSanto, Sr. did not know that O'Brien had taken the list. DeSanto, Sr. did not agree that O'Brien could contact all Desco's customers.

O'Brien filed a declaratory judgment action seeking a judicial decision that the non-compete agreement that he had signed was unenforceable because of inadequacy of consideration. "Consideration" is one of those words that has a different meaning in law than in ordinary conversation and it refers to the compensation or benefit that the promisor will receive when the promise is made. If there is no compensation or benefit to the promisor, associated with making the promise, the promise will not be legally enforceable. Not all promises are legally binding.[19] The common law developed the concept of consideration, so that a promise without consideration is not legally binding and a promise made with consideration is legally binding. Therefore, if O'Brien was not going to receive adequate compensation or benefit for making his promise not to compete, the contract would not be legally binding.

2.2 Judicial decision in the *O'Brien* case

The case was tried on October 30, 2009, before Judge Thomas G. Gavin of the Court of Common Pleas of Chester County, Pennsylvania, sitting as a judge without a jury. Judge Gavin was a very able, highly experienced judge. He graduated from Villanova Law School in 1971. In private practice after graduation, he specialized in civil and criminal litigation. From 1972 through 1975, he was an assistant district attorney. From 1976 through 1981, he was a court-appointed criminal defense attorney. He became a judge in 1986, and he was the president judge of his county court from 1995 to 2000. He retired on January 2, 2011. So, in 2009, when he heard this case, he had extensive trial experience and had served as a judge for more than 20 years.

Judge Gavin, on November 12, 2009, issued a five-page opinion containing findings of fact, conclusions of law, and a discussion providing insight into his reasoning.[20] The only two witnesses mentioned in the opinion are O'Brien and DeSanto, Sr. and the only document referred to is the non-compete agreement.

There were some conflicts in the testimony of the two witnesses. O'Brien testified that he did not read the non-compete agreement before signing it. He also said that he felt that he had to sign the agreement, or he would be fired. He did not consult with an attorney to review the agreement because he thought that DeSanto, Sr. would react negatively to his doing so. DeSanto, Sr. testified that O'Brien did not sign the agreement immediately but, instead, he read it before signing it. He also stated that O'Brien never raised any objection to signing the agreement at any time prior to leaving Desco's employment.

Judge Gavin stated in the opinion that he found some aspects of O'Brien's testimony to not be credible. Specifically, Judge Gavin mentioned that he did not believe that O'Brien had not been informed about the request that he sign a non-compete agreement before it had been presented to him. He also did not find credible O'Brien's statement that DeSanto, Sr. had told O'Brien to "sign or get the f___ out." He did not believe O'Brien's statement that he felt that he had to sign the agreement immediately or be fired and he also did not believe O'Brien's testimony that he could not take the time to read the agreement or to consult with an attorney.[21]

Conversely, Judge Gavin concluded that DeSanto Sr.'s testimony was credible. In particular, Judge Gavin found that DeSanto, Sr. had requested that the non-compete agreement be prepared to protect both Desco and its employees against an employee who might leave and compete with them. Judge Gavin also thought that DeSanto, Sr. had informed O'Brien and the other employees that he was having a non-compete agreement prepared. He also believed DeSanto Sr.'s testimony that O'Brien had appeared to read the non-compete agreement before he signed it. DeSanto Sr. also testified that, while he did not tell O'Brien that he could take the agreement home to read it and/or have an attorney review it, he would not have objected to his doing so.[22]

DeSanto Sr. gave each of the salesmen $500 as consideration for signing the non-compete agreement. Judge Gavin found that DeSanto, Sr.'s testimony was credible when he stated that he selected $500 as the appropriate amount to pay because it represented the average commission on four truckloads of steel.

O'Brien contended that $500 was inadequate consideration for this non-compete agreement because he was being asked to agree not to solicit customers who had generated a six-figure income for him. Judge Gavin stated that he viewed this argument as a convenient "linchpin" (Judge Gavin's choice of word) by which O'Brien was attempting to invalidate the agreement. Notwithstanding that observation, Judge Gavin held that the consideration of $500 for an employee who earned $177,000 in 2006 would appear to be facially inadequate consideration for this non-compete agreement. Judge Gavin, however, did not decide the case on these grounds.

Judge Gavin reasoned: "The law considering covenants not to compete is well-known, as are the rationale for enforcing or not enforcing them."[23] He continued: "Competent counsel can find a case to support just about any position he/she is asserting for or against enforcement of such covenants."[24]

Proceeding to the holding in the case ("the holding" is the reason for the decision), the opinion noted: "The bottom line is that the [non-compete] agreements are generally enforced when shown to be reasonably necessary to protect the employer."[25] In this case, the holding was that the enforcement of the non-compete agreement was not necessary to protect Desco. Judge Gavin explained that "reasonably necessary" was viewed in consideration of the context of time, area and other opportunities available to the employee. There was no question in Judge Gavin's mind that the restrictions in this case were reasonable regarding time and area and that O'Brien was not, in general, prohibited from working in the steel industry.

Judge Gavin, however, found that Desco did not need for its protection even these limited restrictions. Desco had a good relationship with its suppliers that was longer and more established than was O'Brien's. Desco's staying power was based upon its longevity and its strong relationships with its customers. In addition, Desco was able to provide financing to its customers upon favorable terms and offer other inducements for those customers to do business with it. Consequently, Desco did not require the year of protection from O'Brien as a competitor. Enforcement of the restrictive covenant was, therefore, not reasonably necessary.

It is interesting that Judge Gavin took judicial notice (accepted as a fact by the court without testimony being presented regarding that fact) that local and national economies were in desperate condition in 2009 and that two of the most impacted areas of distress were the steel and construction industries in which there were far more sellers than buyers. Desco, notwithstanding the weak economy, by reason of its market position, would still find that its long-term business relationships would ensure the stability of its business. This was the reasoning that led Judge Gavin to decide in favor of O'Brien and against Desco.

Judge Gavin held (made the finding or decided) that the non-compete agreement was not legally binding. O'Brien was not subject to the restrictions contained in the non-compete agreement. He was free to contact Desco's customers and seek their business.

The most surprising aspect of this decision is that Judge Gavin was clearly not pleased with the outcome in this case. Judge Gavin stated the following: "This Judge prefers results that are legally, morally and ethically in sync. Unfortunately, the result here, while legally correct, is morally and ethically offensive. An appropriate alternate caption for this case would be 'no good deed goes unpunished.'"[26]

2.3 Questions about the decision in the *O'Brien* case

I am going to suggest in this book that the criteria for the evaluation of judicial decisions should be correctness, justice and wisdom, which I will define in later chapters. Consequently, my responses to many of the questions that follow will become readily apparent as the reader continues through the chapters.

Meanwhile, the questions that I would like the reader to consider would involve the following issues. How did Judge Gavin decide which decision is correct? In other words, what is the test that he could use and did use to decide that his decision would be correct or incorrect? Since he mentioned that competent lawyers can cite precedents for opposing positions in the case before him, is he suggesting that a decision for Desco as well as the decision for O'Brien would both be correct? If a decision for either side would be correct, would it have been impossible for him to make an incorrect decision?

What criteria would you use to decide that a decision is incorrect? One obvious initial response could be that the judge has attempted to reach a correct decision, but he has been wrong in declaring which legal rule should be applied. There is no such rule, or the applicable rule is different than the one he has pronounced, or he has found the applicable rule, but he has misinterpreted it. I refer to these possibilities as an "incorrect decision by mistake."

If both parties thought that the non-compete agreement was enforceable when it was signed and you could prove this (O'Brien admitted this on cross-examination, for example), would this make a difference in deciding the case? If Desco thought that the agreement was enforceable, and it was reasonable to believe that it was (based, presumably, on the law in Pennsylvania when the agreement was signed), should this have any effect upon the decision? Could Desco claim, then, that a decision against it would have a retroactive effect because it would be contrary to the pre-existing law (the law in existence before the decision was made)?

Suppose for a moment that Judge Gavin had decided that he would reach the moral and/or ethical decision even though that decision would not be, in his judgment, the correct decision. I call this, potentially at least, an "alternate source decision." Is this decision authorized by the pre-existing law, authoritative (it will be a precedent and will become part of the pre-existing law for the next case), and binding (it will resolve the dispute between the parties by favoring one party or the other)? If it would not be binding, what then is the status of the decision regarding the parties? If it is binding on the parties, what should the party who lost the case do when the judge has decided intentionally to make a decision that is contrary to the applicable legal rules? In other words, would this decision favoring the other party justify an appeal to a higher court?

What should then happen on the appeal if O'Brien is the party who appeals, and Judge Gavin had decided in favor of Desco in order to make a moral or ethical decision? Suppose that Judge Gavin had candidly stated that he has reached a moral and/or ethical decision even though he knew that the decision is not consistent with the law that existed prior to the decision being made. Should the appellate court rebuke Judge Gavin for not applying applicable law? Did Judge Gavin have an obligation to apply existing law? If the appellate court does not accept the reason Judge Gavin has given for his decision, such as his desire to make a moral or an ethical decision, are there any acceptable reasons for disregarding applicable law? Would justice qualify as an acceptable reason?

In addition, assume that no appeal is filed, would the alternative decision that is acknowledged to be a moral and/or ethical decision, which is also acknowledged to be inconsistent with existing law, be a binding precedent (binding upon judges deciding future cases)? Or, if it were a decision that is inconsistent with pre-existing law, would it not be a binding precedent because it was inconsistent with pre-existing law? Do the precedents of the pre-existing law, if they are binding precedents, preclude Judge Gavin from avoiding them in making his decision? Does it appear as though Judge Gavin is merely deciding whether to call a ball or a strike?

2.4 Legal philosophies

In this book, and in much more detail in the books that will follow it, I am presenting a legal philosophy that I call creative positivism. I will briefly introduce that legal philosophy in Chapter Ten. I want to discuss other legal philosophies in this book because I will refer to them as I discuss the cases. I have already mentioned the traditional theory, which is the proposition that judges discover the law and never create new legal rules. This theory was discredited by the American Legal Realists, a group of legal theorists who were active in the twentieth century, and the legal positivists.

The leading legal positivist in the twentieth century was H.L.A. Hart who built upon and restructured legal positivism. This theory was prominent in the nineteenth century, and he resuscitated it in the twentieth century. As I mentioned in the introduction, and I will repeat now for those who did not read the introduction, Hart tutored me for one year and supervised my doctoral thesis in the next year when I was a student at Oxford University.

Hart (1907-1992) was the Professor of Jurisprudence at Oxford during the 1950's and 1960's. His classic work is *The Concept of Law*, and this book is still regarded as the most authoritative text for legal positivism.[27] I want to describe some of the terms Hart developed at this point because I will be referring to them in the chapters that follow.

Hart describes the central features of the law and the legal system. The legal system is a normative system. It consists of legal rules that control and facilitate human behavior. The foundation of every legal system is based upon some degree of acceptance by the general population. The acceptance of the law by the society is a social fact.

The fundamental norms of the legal system permit or forbid certain behavior or provide for legal rights to be obtained. The norms must be generally obeyed by the citizenry (those individuals who are subject to the law). I am using the terms "laws," "legal rules" and "norms" as interchangeable terms with the same meaning. The law must provide the rules that set the standards for official behavior and for the creation of new rules.

There are primary rules that govern conduct that Hart calls duty-imposing norms, such as those that provide for which conduct will be prohibited by the criminal laws. A duty imposing norm is addressed to the individuals who are subject to the duty (and indirectly to those to whom the law confers a right to claim that conduct of others should conform to the norm).

There are also power-conferring primary rules that allow members of the society to control their affairs, such as by entering into contracts, getting married and writing wills (with the expectation that if you follow the procedure in the power-conferring rules, your actions will be recognized as legally effective by the relevant governmental officials). When a norm confers a power, the exercising of the power gives rise to reciprocal obligations that allow for the exercising of the power to be effective.

In addition to the primary rules, the legal system will also have secondary rules that establish the procedures by which primary rules are identified, adopted and applied. There must be a generally accepted method for ascertaining which rules are the legally enforceable rules (the valid rules) as distinct from other types of rules (such as those moral rules that are not legally enforceable as legal rules).

The most important of the secondary rules is Hart's rule of recognition which is the generally accepted standard for determining what are the laws that will be applied by the legal officials. The rule of recognition will also identify the legal officials, empower them to act as such, and provide for the procedures they must follow in order to perform their duties and exercise their legal authority.

Another secondary rule is the rule of change by which the primary rules may be adopted, altered, modified, expanded, contracted and deleted. The third secondary rule is the rule of adjudication which is the established system in the society according to which lawsuits may be initiated in order to resolve disputes, address laws which are violated and provide for rights to be asserted. In the adjudication process, the laws may be applied, interpreted and, pursuant to the rule of change, modified.

While I accept Hart's legal theory as the basis for beginning one's understanding of the law and the legal system, I would modify its provisions to a limited extent to clarify some of the aspects of the way the law actually operates. This brief introduction is not the place where I want to pursue these details.

My primary disagreement with Hart's description of the legal system is regarding the judicial process generally and the discretion that judges and other legal officials may exercise in performing their duties. This is the next subject that I will address, and it really strikes at the heart of both my rejection of this aspect of Hart's legal philosophy and my disapproval of the analogy of judges acting like umpires.

2.5 Judicial discretion

Some legal theorists assert that judges are not authorized to make alternate source decisions; in other words, judges have no discretion to avoid applying applicable law. In fact, according to the traditional theory, every decision is correct because it is based upon legal rules that existed before the decision was made. The judge just applies the pre-existing law, without exercising any discretion, to the facts in the case and the outcome is obvious and indisputable. Judges just look for the law and apply it. They do not create the law. Some judges even claim, like Chief Justice Roberts and Justice Kavanaugh, that they perform their judicial role in a manner which is like the role of umpires in a baseball game and all they do, in deciding cases, is the equivalent of the umpire calling balls and strikes.

There are other theorists who contend that judges have limited discretion. Judges will be presented with many cases in which the result will be clear and judges exercise discretion only when the law is indeterminate or unclear. According to a similar view, discretion is exercised only where there are gaps in the law. While there can be mistakes (the incorrect decisions by mistake, which will be discussed in Chapter Four), there are no situations where the judge, according to the traditional theory and to some legal positivists, intentionally makes an alternate source decision because he would prefer to make a just or wise decision (or, in Judge Gavin's terms, a moral or ethical decision).

Therefore, according to some legal philosophers, the judge either makes a correct decision or exercises discretion to make a decision that cannot be characterized as correct or incorrect. I contend that there is a potential correct decision in every case, but the judge does not make a correct decision in every case. She may make an incorrect decision by mistake. She also has the authority to make an alternate source decision.

Some philosophers claim that judges have unlimited discretion. They maintain that there are no correct decisions because judges never decide cases in accordance with pre-existing law. According to this view, judges always attempt to make, as one possibility, just and/or wise decisions. In the most extreme version of this theory, if you want to understand how decisions are made, you must study the psychology of the judge's decision-making process. In a less extreme view, the legal rules are too uncertain for it to make sense to study whether the decisions are correct, and we should focus on what courts really do (the empirical study of judicial behavior). I contend that judges may, and usually do, make correct decisions.

The extent to which Judge Gavin had discretion in making the ultimate decision in the O'Brien case could depend, as some theorists would maintain, upon how settled the pre-existing law was when he made the decision. Judge Gavin mentioned that competent counsel could cite cases for both positions—the non-compete agreement is enforceable or is not enforceable. Therefore, one might conclude that there could be multiple correct decisions. Or, alternatively, there could be no correct decision.

Judge Gavin, sitting as a judge without a jury, had to make findings of fact based upon the credibility of witnesses. He also had to interpret the non-compete agreement. After resolving these issues, the question remains: did Judge Gavin also have discretion in deciding whether he should find that the non-compete agreement was enforceable?

Some theorists have contended that the judge has authority to disregard the pre-existing law and to decide cases based upon other sources that would be acceptable in the reaching of judicial decisions.

Other theorists characterize all sources other than the pre-existing law as extra-legal.

Among these alternate sources could be moral and/or ethical rules. In addition, Judge Gavin could consider principles that form the basis for the legal rules. Judge Gavin mentioned morals, ethics, and specific principles in his opinion, but it is not clear what impact, if any, these potential sources had on the decision. Some theorists have contended that all these sources, and other potential sources, are and should be considered by judges in making their decisions.[28]

Another potential source to be considered in making decisions beside morals and ethics could be justice. In other words, judges may strive to reach just decisions, and Judge Gavin may have considered whether his decision would be just. In fact, Judge Gavin appeared to be displeased with the outcome of the case. Is he suggesting that an appellate court should reverse his decision? Would he, if he were an appellate judge, reach a different result?

Would a decision for Desco be just because Desco invested capital in training O'Brien? Desco gave O'Brien access to its list of customers, and Desco agreed, even though it did not have to do so and it was contrary to its interests, that O'Brien could do business with the customers O'Brien had developed. Alternatively, would a decision for O'Brien be just because O'Brien should be allowed to pursue his occupation and O'Brien could not effectively compete with Desco anyway?

Moreover, this decision, like virtually all published decisions, will be a precedent. Therefore, the rule established in this case could control the outcome of future cases and could be considered by lawyers in advising clients and by clients in making decisions. The consequences of this decision as a precedent could, then, have been a decisive factor in the decision that Judge Gavin reached. The decision in the *O'Brien v. Desco* case is now part of the pre-existing law for the next case, and, since Judge Gavin is creating a precedent, we cannot avoid the conclusion that Judge Gavin is exercising creative judgment.

Judge Gavin could also have decided that the consideration was inadequate to render the non-compete agreement enforceable. Yet he did not. Why not? Why did he prefer to base his decision on the enforcement of the promise not to compete not being "reasonably necessary" to protect Desco? Does this decision, then, as a precedent provide guidance to lawyers in drafting non-compete agreements in the future? Should Judge Gavin have indicated how much consideration would be adequate so that lawyers in the future would know how to advise their clients for their clients to enter into enforceable non-compete agreements?

Would it have made a difference in the outcome of this case if testimony had been introduced by Desco that the lawyer who drafted this non-compete agreement had researched the law prior to doing so and had relied upon decisions made by courts, decisions that "obligated" Judge Gavin to decide that the non-compete agreement was valid and binding upon O'Brien? Research of the law would have revealed that non-compete agreements between employers and employees are valid if they are reasonable regarding the time period, the geographical area and description of the business that is protected from competition and only if adequate consideration is paid and the agreement is economically necessary to protect the employer. Reasonableness of the agreement was not raised in this case, so we may assume that the parties agreed that the terms of the restriction were reasonable.

Judge Gavin mentioned the state of the economy in his opinion. But how could the lawyer who drafted the agreement have anticipated the state of the economy years after the non-compete agreement was drafted? Maybe, the non-compete agreement would have been valid and binding in a different economic environment. Does this mean that the state of the economy is a factor to be considered in drafting non-compete agreements and in courts determining their validity?

How would the lawyer drafting the non-compete agreement determine if the restriction is economically necessary for Desco? Does the economic necessity change if the economy changes? How can the lawyer gauge economic necessity in five years or ten years?

This brings us to what I am calling "the wise decision." Should Judge Gavin have considered the consequences of his decision on the development of the law regarding the enforcement of non-compete agreements? In other words, should he have been concerned with whether enforcing non-compete agreements will or will not promote competition, encourage or discourage employers from providing training to new employees, promote or restrict employers in providing access to confidential lists of customers, and provide a rationale for greater or lesser use of non-compete agreements? Are these consequences of his decision that Judge Gavin should have considered?

Was Judge Gavin influenced by, or a victim of, capitalistic economic thinking in making his decision? In other words, did he conclude that there was no economic necessity for the non-compete agreement to be enforced because he accepted that the legal rules are designed to enhance capital growth and capital growth occurs when competition is fostered and supported?

Should it have made a difference in the decision if O'Brien was not a single self-employed individual but he, instead, went to work for a large competitor of Desco? If Desco were less successful, should the decision have been for Desco? Should Judge Gavin not have considered these factors because to do so creates uncertainty in the law and in the prediction of how cases will be decided?

To what extent, then, is certainty in the law a factor to be considered in the making of judicial decisions? Is it important that there be certainty in the law so that citizens can rely upon the law in making decisions about how they should conduct their business? Do lawyers require certainty in the law in order to advise clients what specific acts will be legal or illegal, what contracts will be enforceable or unenforceable and how they will be able to rely upon the law?

Did Judge Gavin make a pragmatic decision, and, if he did not, should he have done so? Some legal theorists have contended that judges should always make pragmatic decisions.

Other legal theorists endorse a theory promoting law as integrity. What does it mean to consider integrity? Is a decision that disregards integrity not a correct decision? Or, once again, when all these theories are considered, should we conclude that it is not possible for a judge to make a correct decision? Or the same question looked at from a different point of view, is it possible for a judge to make an incorrect decision, such as when the judge makes a mistake in applying the pre-existing law? Also, does the judge make an incorrect decision when the judge concludes that it would be preferable to make a just and/or wise decision?

I had the privilege of discussing the decision in the O'Brien case with Judge Gavin on January 19, 2012, in his chambers in the Chester County Courthouse in West Chester, Pennsylvania. I asked him many of the questions that I have asked in this chapter, and I will present his answers to these questions in Appendix A.

According to the traditional theory (the theory apparently relied upon by Chief Justice Roberts and Justice Kavanaugh for their view that judges are like umpires), there is no basis for discussing the alternate source decision. Their view is that judges strive only to make correct decisions. I maintain that, in order to appreciate correct decisions, you must consider decisions that do not qualify as correct decisions. In short, there are no correct decisions unless there are also potentially incorrect decisions. The opposite is also true—there can be no incorrect decisions if there are no correct decisions. Before we tackle incorrect decisions, we should describe the correct decision, which is the subject of Section 3.6 in the next chapter.

More by coincidence than by design, we will consider several cases involving contracts. Every mature legal system has provisions for contracts. If there were no rules enabling contracts to be formed, you would be unable to distinguish a non-enforceable promise from a legally binding promise. When you take a job, you enter into an unwritten or written employment contract. When you marry, there is a contract of marriage.

In the following chapters, we will consider a contract to provide insurance if the insured party causes damages by pollution (Chapter Four), a contract to pay someone who has saved the promisor's life (Chapter Five), a commercial contract to pay a debt (Chapter Six), a contract for the exclusive rights to provide taxi services at a train station (Chapter Six) and many other types of contracts.

Before considering all these other contract cases, let's first see if we can define the correct decision.

3.
DEFINING THE CORRECT DECISION

The correct decision is the starting point for the study of judicial decisions. In order to agree upon what a correct decision is, we have to consider several concepts: (1) we should distinguish judging from other forms of decision-making; (2) we should look at judging in the judicial process; (3) we should clarify what is involved in making a rational, reasoned judicial decision; (4) we need to identify the standard that is used in making correct judicial decisions; and (5) we must clarify how the law can simultaneously be certain and changing.

3.1 Judging apples

You start a new job at an apple orchard. It is your job to sort the apples for sale to the customers. You are told that there are four categories: best, good, tasty and fine. The best apples are sold to the companies that compile gift baskets. The good apples are sold to the largest customers—supermarket chains. The tasty apples are sold to the smaller customers—produce stores, farmer's markets, convenience stores, small grocery stores. The fine apples are sold to the companies that make applesauce. You are shown examples of the four classes of apples and are informed that the criteria are size, color, lack of blemishes and shape. You're now an apple judge.

After your first week, your boss tells you that you should strive for a minimum of 20 percent of the apples classified as best and a maximum of 10 percent classified as fine. Now, you are not just grading apples, but you are also performing the task with your thumb on the scale (or grading on a curve). You continue to apply the criteria given to you, but the criteria have been modified. You're still an apple judge.

Suppose that there is an early frost that damages the crop and that this adversely impacts the quality of the apples you are judging. If you are going to apply the grading criteria, but given the poor quality of this harvest, circumstances have resulted in the modified criteria providing for questionable results.

If the crop is sufficiently damaged that, if you had been applying the original grading criteria, you might find only one percent of the apples are best and over 50 percent are fine. You may conclude that you could be supplying your customers with apples that are substantially inferior to those that they have purchased earlier in the year based upon the modified criteria. You may conclude that you should inform your boss of your concern that the customers will be disappointed with the apples they receive. You could view this as a question of suitable business practices, or you might even consider it to be a moral issue—you are not comfortable with delivering apples that are so inferior to those previously sold.

I want to use this simple example to establish some basic points about the process of judging:

First, in order to judge, you must start with criteria because this is a systematic process.

Second, applying the criteria is a reasoning process (judgment is required) as distinct from a chaotic and undisciplined procedure.

Third, there are rules of procedure that control how you go about performing the judging process.

3.2 The judging process

For a judge to judge, and not just issue decrees, he must go through a process that would allow us to call what he is doing "judging." This is not based upon an empirical study of how judges decide cases. It is a description of what a judge would have to do in a judicial process that would allow us to conclude that the judge is judging. The judge, if he is acting in accordance with the customary norms prescribing what a judge must do in order to perform his duties, must judge cases and not just announce results in cases.

Consider an extreme example. Suppose that a judge decided cases before him by flipping coins. Heads would result in a verdict for the plaintiff (the plaintiff is the person or entity who initiated the case) and tails would result in a verdict for the defendant (the defendant is the person or entity being sued or the accused party in a criminal case). Suppose further that the judge has a very astute law clerk who is capable of writing an opinion for the judge to sign that, on its face, reads like opinions written by judges who actually judge cases. The law clerk can also tailor the fact-finding involved in deciding the case to be consistent with the result determined by the coin toss. It may not even be shocking if the reversal rate by the appellate courts for this judge on appeals from his decisions is not significantly different from that of his colleagues.

I believe that it is indisputable that the judge in my example is not actually judging cases in the sense in which we think of judges deciding cases. There may be no canonical rule prohibiting a judge from flipping coins as part of his procedure of making his decisions. But, nevertheless, we would find it disturbing if this was the procedure he was employing (just as we would if the judge was accepting bribes). He is not judging cases, just as our employee in the apple orchard would not be grading the apples if he put the first apple, and the fifth apple, and the ninth apple, and the thirteenth apple in the bin for the best apples.

This book pays homage to the making of the correct decision.[29] I want to emphasize the correct decision because I believe that the concept of the correct decision is the foundation upon which to build a plausible legal philosophy about the judicial process.

3.3 Judging in general

Judging presupposes that you are making a rational decision by application of criteria that you will use in making the decision. It is a reasoning process. We make many decisions that we would not regard as "judging." Judging is not deciding whether you prefer vanilla or chocolate ice cream, would rather watch a movie than a football game, or decide to take a walk in the park before you make dinner.

Judging requires the use of criteria. We may disagree about the criteria for judging in at least two different significant ways. We could question whether the appropriate criteria have been used. We could agree upon the criteria but disagree about how the criteria have been interpreted or applied. When the apple orchard owner tells you that no more than ten percent of the apples can be considered to be fine (the lowest category for judging apples), you may conclude that this as an unwarranted (unfair, immoral) change in the criteria. But I think that there is general agreement regarding judging that there must be criteria that are considered by the judge (the reasons for the decision), and applying the criteria must constitute a rational (logical) process.

In order to have a correct decision, you must have a standard by which correctness may be determined. Therefore, we must establish what the standard will be. Since we are discussing judicial decisions, and judges sit in a court of law, the starting port for this voyage is to look at the law.

Law is a systematic network of legal rules. (I previously mentioned, I use the terms "rules," "norms" and "laws" interchangeably). The rules are utilized to control behavior, to form the basis for rights and liberties and they are applied to resolve disputes. Rules are general in nature and formulated so that they are available to provide for dictated results to a variety of factual situations either inherent in the rule itself or demonstrated in previous applications of the rule in prior decisions. Application of the rule is based upon the terms in the rule.

The correct decision is a decision in which the applicable rule is applied, and the rule is not altered when it is applied in any significant or material way. The correct decision, then, is the rational application of a pre-existing legal rule (derived from the pre-existing law which is the law in existence before the decision was reached). It does not involve any reason for applying the law other than the legal rule that is applied is the appropriate rule within the law to be applied to the factual situation being considered. It is sufficient if the act in question falls logically within the scope of the rule. No other reason is required for applying the applicable rule.

If the otherwise applicable rule is not applied, or a new rule is created, there must be a reason for doing so. In addition, the reason must be an acceptable reason. There are customary rules that govern the acceptability of the reason for deviating from applying the otherwise applicable rule to decide the case. As I will discuss below, the judicial decision to be viewed as acceptable must be a rational, reasoned decision. For present purposes, the point that I am making is that the correct decision is made when the applicable legal rule of the pre-existing law is applied to the factual situation in question, the factual situation falls within the scope of the rule, and the rule need not be altered to be so applied.

The law, however, is not static. It is subject to change, including changes made by judges in making judicial decisions. Because the law is constantly being changed, it may appear to be unstable, and unsatisfactory as a criterion for making decisions because of its indeterminacy. The law, however, may be both determinate and changeable. I use the analogy of buying and selling a house to explain how this may occur.

3.4 Analogy of buying and selling a house

There is a sense in which every published decision may change the law. Even a correct decision will change the law, but the change may not be a material change. The analogy I want to propose is that, if you buy a house and then sell the house you bought, it is never exactly the same house, even if both events occur on the same day.[30]

If the two transactions occur on the same day, and you go from the settlement at which you purchased the house to the settlement at which you will sell the house you just purchased, and never even enter the house or take direct possession of it, the purchase and the sale are not the exact same factual situation even though they involve the very same house. First, if you were the first owner of the house when you purchased it (the house has just been built and it is a new house), the purchaser from you is not the first owner but is the second owner. If you were the first owner, when the purchaser from you sells the house in this hypothetical example, it will have had two prior owners and not just one. As will be clear when we consider the *Conway* case in Chapter Seven, there may be legal consequences that are the result of being the first owner rather than a subsequent owner.

Secondly, the prices could be different. But, even if the prices are the same, you now have two sales of the house with two different sellers and two different purchasers, all of whom impliedly agree that the fair market value of the house is the same figure. There are now two "comparable sales" (sales of comparable properties to the property that is being appraised) that can be used in an appraisal to arrive at the fair market value of this house or a similar house.

In the more typical case, you will own the house for a few years or more. When you sell the house, assuming that you have made no changes in the house or to the lot the house is on, all of the appliances and fixtures are now a few years older (and, therefore, have a few years less of useful life). Some other houses in the neighborhood may have sold during your tenure as an owner and now the composition of the neighborhood and the characteristics of the neighbors will have changed. There could also be changes in the larger neighborhood, like a new shopping center opened nearby or a new landfill is now in the vicinity.

The real estate taxes will probably have changed, since they are usually increasing. The tax assessments in the neighborhood could now reflect the price paid in various sales transactions and this could change the market value of your house in comparison to similar houses in the neighborhood that have or have not changed owners recently.

The paint on the house may now look more tired, the grass may be greener or browner and your children and domestic animals may have contributed to the appearance of the house. You may have made changes that have improved the house or improved it in your opinion but not in the opinion of the marketplace. Notwithstanding these potential changes, you are selling the house that you purchased.

Judicial decisions in developing the law are similar to the situation of the house. The facts in the precedent (the earlier decision that contains the legal rule that the judge is considering applying to decide the case before him) and the facts in the instant case will never be exactly the same, though the differences may be immaterial. Just as every house is unique; no two cases are identical. The factual situation in every case is also unique. In comparing the instant case with a relevant precedent, the social factors will be different, the parties will be different, and the judge is likely to be different. The second decision, even if the wording of the legal rule does not change, is a reaffirmation of the rule, reinforcing it and strengthening it. Circumstances will have changed, but the rule may still be the same rule.

The non-material changes in the law are like the sale of the house that is the same house on the same lot, but it is not exactly the same house you purchased. It may have changed not because of any action you took but because of the passage of time and the difference in circumstances (the neighborhood, the economy, the interest rate, political decisions that have been made, etc.). Even though different, the house you are selling continues to be the same house that you bought.

Similarly, the case the judge is deciding may be very much like a previous decision he or another judge has made. But there will be differences. Some, maybe most, possibly all, of the differences may be immaterial. The judge may declare that the rule of the precedent applies to her case, which makes the decision appear to be almost automatic ("mechanical" or "formalistic"). The differences may be material, but not significant enough to avoid applying the pre-existing law and the rule itself does not change when it is applied. But, when she applies the law to this case, the judge is creating a new precedent. Therefore, even though the law is stable, while the rule may not change, the law may achieve greater clarity.

As mentioned above, the correct decision, even though it is correct in its application of pre-existing law, it will enhance the law by creating more certainty in the law. Incorrect decisions will change the law. Both the incorrect decision by mistake and the decision when the pre-existing law is intentionally not applied will change the law. The questions for the judge, the lawyers, the parties and anyone else who is a potential critic of the judicial decision are still whether the judicial decision was correct or incorrect.

3.5 Reasons for changing the law

The law consists of the legal rules. The acceptable reasons for judicial decisions in which the pre-existing law is not applied, which I will describe as justice and wisdom, are not sources of the law. They are sources for judicial decisions in the sense that the norms of acceptable behavior in judicial decision-making empower, permit and authorize judges to create new legal rules that they may apply in deciding cases.

Justice and wisdom are standards for evaluating law, but they are not part of the law. Therefore, "just" and "wise" are external standards of evaluation, while also being internal sources for making judicial decisions. When considered in addition to the law, such as, for example, in making a judicial decision, the alternate sources are incorporated into the decision-making process. As standards of justification and evaluation, they remain outside of the law, unless they are specifically incorporated into the legal rules (for example, "just cause" or "bad faith").

The alternate source decision could be justified if it is a just decision and/or a wise decision, and the just decision and/or the wise decision is more desirable than the correct decision in a particular case. A judicial decision must be principled in the sense that it can be justified only by an appeal to a pre-existing legal rule or by a reason that overrides applying the pre-existing legal rule. This reason might be called an extra-legal consideration in the sense that the reason (justice or wisdom, as I am defining these terms) is not part of the pre-existing law.

Using justice or wisdom as the source for a judicial decision is not really an extra-legal consideration because the rules of the legal system authorize consideration of justice and wisdom (as I will describe them, Chapter Five for the just decision and Chapter Six for the wise decision), to be acceptable reasons for judicial decisions. In the same way, the legal system requires that a judicial decision be a rational, reasoned decision. As part of the legal system, this requirement is also not extra-legal. In short, justice and wisdom as sources for judicial decisions are not extra-legal for the same reason that deciding cases by flipping coins would be extra-legal. These rules of the legal system are established in written and unwritten customary norms that may or may not be incorporated into the law.

In summary, the legal system contains norms that prescribe how judicial decisions should be made. These norms prescribe that judges must make rational, reasoned decisions based upon the pre-existing law or justified by looking to alternate sources for making such decisions which I am describing as justice or wisdom. These norms require that judges make correct decisions rather than decisions that are not rational or reasoned. The acceptable reasons for making judicial decisions are the application of the pre-existing law (the correct decision) or applying the alternate sources (justice and wisdom). Our next task, then, is to further describe the rational, reasoned judicial decision which may or may not qualify as the correct decision.[31]

3.6 The rational, reasoned judicial decision.

Applying the legal rule to the factual situation presented to the judge in order to make the correct decision is a rational, reasoned process. It is not an evaluative process. These two points—the decision is rational and reasoned but it is not evaluative—are the fundamental foundation for the definition of the correct decision. The correct decision is not the subject of evaluation by any criterion other than its correctness. Evaluation of the desirability of the judicial decision, as distinct from whether the correct decision has been reached, is based upon criteria other than correctness. In contrast to the correct decision not being an evaluative process, fact-finding is an evaluative process seeking truth. Fact-finding is part of the process that will lead to the correct decision when the judge finds and applies the applicable legal rule in making the decision. Finding the applicable legal rule is an analytical process. Applying the legal rule to the factual situation is a rational process, more or less like logical reasoning.

The judicial decision may be rational but unreasoned or reasoned but not rational. The legal rule may be applied, and the decision may be rational because it is not regarded as being an instance of logical incoherence. It is rational because it is logical. The criteria for rationality are the rules of logic. But the decision may still be unreasoned.

The decision must be based upon a rule of the pre-existing law in order to be a correct decision. In other words, the reason for the judge deciding for the plaintiff (the party who initiated the suit) must be the application of an existing rule for the decision to be declared to be a correct decision. The correct decision does not involve evaluation of the rule. It is sufficient if the act in question falls logically within the scope of the rule.

If the rule is not applied, and a new rule is created, the decision may be a good decision (a desirable decision), even though it is no longer considered to be a correct decision. This is where evaluation enters the judicial process. In making the correct decision, the judge is not engaging in evaluation of the legal rule. He determines the content of the legal rule without thinking about what the law should be. Without evaluating the law, the judge can determine what the law is. I will expand upon this point in Chapters Nine and Ten.

Making the rational, reasoned decision does not mean that the judicial process is mechanical. Judicial creativity may be involved in finding the applicable legal rule. I do not have the space to discuss legal reasoning in this book. I will discuss reasoning by analogy and other forms of legal reasoning in *The Judge and the Philosopher*.

In considering judicial decisions, you must appreciate that the judge must decide the case that is presented to her, and she must consider what legal rule would be applicable to do so. Courts are not legislatures. Judges do not decide to change the law on their own. They must act upon cases that have been filed. Judges do not initiate cases and do not offer advisory opinions on hypothetical cases. They have no control over the flow of cases filed in court. They have no roving agenda to develop new areas of the law.

This book pays homage to the correct decision.[32] The correct decision is a decision that is made by application of pre-existing law. I do not mean that the decision does not change the law. To a very limited degree, as I have mentioned, almost every published decision will change the law. But the making of all decisions, review of all decisions, and evaluation of all decisions must start with the correct decision.

There is no sense in discussing changes in the law made by decisions without acknowledging that there is pre-existing law that could have been applied to make the correct decision. Just as every voyage must start from a single port, so every case must be decided, and every case can be decided, by application of pre-existing law. Once again, the correct decision is the port from which this voyage starts.

This does not ignore the vast difference between cases in which the law is very determinate, and its application is almost unavoidable and incontrovertible and cases in which there is great uncertainty and opposing lawyers are each making arguments that are compelling. Remember that Judge Gavin said in the *O'Brien* case that convincing arguments could be made for both the plaintiff and the defendant. But a decision must be made. In this sense, judicial decision-making is like the umpire calling balls and strikes. The pitch is either a ball or a strike, though it might be a very close call. The umpire cannot refuse to decide because it is too close to call.

Similarly, the judge can find in the pre-existing law the rule that allows him to decide the case even if he decides that there is no cause of action that supports the plaintiff's claim (no legal rule that provides for the plaintiff to have a claim) or that he does not have jurisdiction to hear the case or that the case is frivolous, he is making a decision in the case.[33] When he is deciding the case, the judge at some point must consider the correct decision, even if the judge does not like the result of making the correct decision and will ultimately decide not to reach the correct decision.

Judges may misinterpret the statute or the precedent and reach an incorrect decision because they have made a mistake. If the judge realizes that the proposed decision will be a mistake, he must find the alternative decision that he believes would not be a mistake. It is not consistent with the structural integrity of the legal system (its coherence, completeness, comprehensiveness and internal consistency) to maintain that a decision for either the plaintiff or the defendant would be correct. The structure of the legal system does not accommodate that view because the judge must decide the case and, if he is applying the law, it is not possible that a decision for either the plaintiff or the defendant could both be correct.

I recognize that it is possible for the plaintiff to prevail on some claims and not on others or that there could be a decision holding some defendants liable but not others. Also, the plaintiff may not get a result that the plaintiff views as adequate compensation. Similarly, a defendant may be found guilty on some charges but not on others. In a close case (you can call it a hard case, if you like), there can be a serious disagreement about which decision would be the correct decision. Each of the combatants could make an argument for what they claim is a correct decision.

The correct decision is presumptively justified. This means that the judge is always justified in applying the pre-existing law to decide the case. No other reason than the pre-existing law need be proffered for the decision. The judge is also justified in making the just decision and/or the wise decision if that will result in a better decision than the correct decision. The correct decision may also be the just decision and/or the wise decision.

It is difficult to define which reasons would be justifiable for judicial decisions, but I will provide examples of actual cases to aid in defining the just decision and the wise decision. Justification requires objective reasons rather than subjective reasons. The reasons must be stated in language that relates to and references the factual situation and indicates, directly or indirectly which facts are relevant and why they are relevant. The decision-making process cannot be separated from the justificatory process.[34]

While "just" and "wise" are, admittedly, vague terms, there is some generally agreed-upon understanding in the usage of these terms. These terms have enough of a basic commonality of understanding in a specific jurisdiction with a mature legal system at a particular time that they can be discussed in a meaningful way. I will attempt to describe how I use these terms in the following chapters.

3.7 Using the law

We are discussing a specific kind of judging–the judging that is involved in the judicial process. I am using "judicial process," in an expansive sense. There are many different types of courts (I will list only those with which I have had personal experience): small claims courts; justices of the peace; municipal courts; arbitration proceedings (both as part of the judicial system and separate from the judicial system); appellate institutions associated with administrative agencies (environmental hearing board, for example); juvenile courts; domestic relations courts; orphan's courts, commercial courts; traffic courts; military courts; and civil and criminal trial and appellate courts.

I would include as judging the decisions reached by arbitrators, administrative agencies, quasi-judicial bodies (zoning hearing boards, for example) and judicial officials. While I believe that police officers make similar decisions in deciding whether a crime has been committed, or whether to make an arrest, and the decisions are reasoned decisions, and criteria are being applied, these decisions often must be made in a hasty fashion. Therefore, they may not rise to the degree of reasoning that would be required to consider them to be the result of judicial or quasi-judicial reasoning. Moreover, some decision makers do not have to write opinions with reasons to support their decisions. Arbitrators may just announce awards. Courts may enter *per curium* decisions (decision for the court without naming a judge as the author).

The law that officials use in making judicial decisions is a set of concrete rules within a specific legal system at a specific time. There can be a legal system that is no longer operative (in force anywhere) but still exists in a conceptual sense. We can discuss the application of Roman law to a particular situation, even though Roman law no longer exists as valid law anywhere in our world. We can explain why there would be a different result if German law were applied rather than French law.

A lawyer advising a client about whether an action contemplated by the client would be a legal act is going through a reasoning process somewhat similar to that which a judge might employ. The lawyer, like the judge, will consider the legal rules and will apply those rules to a specific factual situation. The lawyer, in a sense, is trying to anticipate what a judge would decide if a judge had to consider whether the legal rules prohibited the act in question. The lawyer may also advise the client how to accomplish the desired result without violating the law.

When we speak of the current law, we are always considering a temporal and a spatial context for the law. When a lawyer writes a contract, he is, to a certain extent, not only trying to apply the current law in drafting the provisions of the contract but also trying to anticipate what the law might be if the contract becomes the subject of litigation next year or in 20 years.

The lawyer must also consider where the potential litigation might occur, and which legal system's laws will likely be applied to resolve the litigation. The jurisdiction where the case is heard could look to another jurisdiction's legal system and apply the laws of another legal system. The law in one jurisdiction may call for the law of another jurisdiction to be applied in certain cases. The contract may state which legal system's laws will be applicable, and the applicable law will be applied in the event that the contract has to be interpreted. The contract may also stipulate which method of decision making will be employed (arbitration, judge without a jury, jury trial) to decide litigation about the contract.

There could be a retroactive result if the current law (the pre-existing law when the case is heard) is not applied to decide the case but a new legal rule is created to decide the case. If the draftsman of the contract anticipates a change in the law when the case will be heard in a few years, there is a prospective aspect to the drafting of the contractual provision. These issues of retroactive application and anticipatory expectation always create some difficulty in drafting a contract. The contract may specify that a change in the law will not apply to interpretation of the contract.

Once again, though, there is pre-existing law that will be a controlling influence in the outcome of the case if a correct decision is reached. The pre-existing law is the law in that jurisdiction when the case is decided. The current law at the time the contract is drafted will be the same as the pre-existing law if the law does not change during the interval between drafting of the contract and interpretation of the contract by a judicial official.

A lawyer acting as an advocate after the event has occurred and the lawsuit has been filed is going to try to convince the judge that the legal rules that would be applicable to the facts that she wants to establish as the relevant facts should result in a judgment in favor of her client. The opposing counsel will be arguing for different rules, or a different interpretation of the rules, or for the finding of facts that would support his client's version of the case. From the perspective of both advocates, they will often claim that the decision they are proposing is the correct decision, with one important qualification.

One of the lawyers could propose that the court reach a decision that is inconsistent with the pre-existing law. I am not referring here to an argument that the court should make a mistake. Rather, the argument could be that the court should reach a decision that is not a correct decision but is a just decision or a decision with better consequences. In both instances, the argument presupposes that the decision is based upon a change in the rules being applied to make the decision. The position that I am taking requires an extended explanation because it will appear on the surface to be contrary to what an advocate would do.

When I use the term "the incorrect decision," I know that some confusion results from the use of that term. Put aside the situation where a mistake is made. I am also using this term as a term of art with a specific meaning to refer to the situation in which the advocate is arguing that application of the pre-existing rules will result in a gross injustice, or the rule of the pre-existing law will have undesirable consequences and the rule should be changed. Calling this an incorrect decision may at first blush seem odd.

In many situations, maybe in almost all situations, the advocate will not explicitly suggest a change in the rules. Rather, the advocate will attempt to interpret the rules in a way in which, if you apply her interpretation, the case will be decided in favor of her client. The judge, or the law professor, or the law student or the opposing advocate may conclude that the interpretation being urged upon the court is not the correct interpretation of the legal rules in the statute or in the precedents. They will suggest that the correct decision would not be in favor of the initial advocate's client.[35]

When you argue that a particular interpretation is not accurate, it would follow that, if the inaccurate interpretation is accepted, there will necessarily be what I am referring to as an incorrect decision. If that decision would be an incorrect decision, then you must have in mind an alternate decision that you would contend would be a correct decision or an alternate decision, even if it also would be an incorrect decision, that would result in a better decision.

The advocate may argue for a decision that would not be consistent with the pre-existing law because applying the pre-existing law would result in an undesirable outcome. He is urging the court not to reach a correct decision (though he may couch the argument in language that does not make that explicit assertion).

The most important difference between the apple judge and the judicial judge is that the judge in a court of law is not only judging the subject of his decision (the case before him) but he may also be judging the law itself, the criteria for his decision. In short, he is not only judging the case, but he is judging the law, and, unlike the apple judge who cannot change the criteria for his judgment (he is like the umpire), the judge in court may change the criteria he uses to make his decision.

The advocate may also argue for a correct decision that would also be a just decision or a wise decision. In other words, there is some overlap between these three elements of the judicial decision. The interpretation of the legal rule may be influenced by the judge's desire to reach a just decision and/or a wise decision and such result could be consistent with his interpretation of the pre-existing law. If you agree with the judge's interpretation, you are agreeing that he is reaching a correct decision.

All of this presupposes that there is a pre-existing law that is sufficiently determinate (certain and predictable) that it is sensible to discuss that applying the rules of the pre-existing law will allow the judge to reach a correct decision.

A judicial decision, regardless of whether it is correct or incorrect, may be authorized, authoritative and binding. It will be binding upon the parties if the judge who makes the decision is authorized to make it and it is made in accordance with the rules of the legal system. As I will explain in *The Judge and the President*, the decision will be authoritative if it is published. The decision will be valid only if the judge has the legal authority to make the decision. As I will explain in the next chapter, it is important to distinguish the validity of the decision from the correctness of the decision.

4.
THE INCORRECT DECISION

CINCINNATI INSURANCE COMPANY V. FLANDERS ELECTRIC MOTOR SERVICE, INC—AN INCORRECT DECISION BY MISTAKE

4.1 Factual situation in the *Cincinnati* case

Flanders Electric Motor Service, Inc. ("Flanders") operated its business following contemporary environmental standards. The company sold and repaired motors and other equipment at its facility in Indiana. From 1971 to 1988, Flanders sent electrical transformers that had to be repaired to Missouri Electrics Works ("MEW") in Cape Girardeau, Missouri. Some of these transformers may have contained fluids contaminated with PCBs.[36]

In the mid-1980's, the Environmental Protection Agency ("EPA:") conducted an investigation of the MEW site and found substantial PCB contamination caused by inadequate and improper handling and storage practices. This practice resulted in the gradual release of waste materials, pollutants or other contaminants over a period of 20 years. The EPA notified the 600 customers that sent transformers to MEW, including Flanders, that they could be found to be responsible for environmental remediation costs.

Fortunately, Flanders had purchased insurance from Cincinnati Insurance Co. ("Insurance Co.") to cover property damage claims.

Flanders notified Insurance Co. of the possible claim that could result from the EPA investigation. Flanders believed that Insurance Co. had to defend it and to indemnify it (pay on its behalf) against any property damage claims arising from pollution of the MEW site. Under the terms of the pollution exclusion clause in the insurance policy, however, there was no insurance coverage for property damage arising from pollution except in one narrow set of circumstances, to wit, if the release of pollutants could be characterized as "sudden and accidental." Specifically, the insurance policy provided that the "exclusion [from insurance coverage] does not apply if such discharge, dispersal, release or escape is sudden and accidental." In other words, there is insurance coverage only if the pollution is caused by a sudden and accidental event.

The Insurance Co. denied insurance coverage to Flanders, asserting that the pollution did not qualify as "sudden and accidental." The Insurance Co. filed a declaratory judgment action in the Federal District Court in Indiana (S.D. Indiana, Evansville Division) seeking a court order supporting its contention. A declaratory judgment action is a case in which a plaintiff is seeking a court decision resolving a controversy between the plaintiff and the defendant, which in this case would be a decision that the plaintiff did in fact have insurance coverage for the discharge at the MEW site that caused the pollution. O'Brien had also filed a declaratory judgment action against Desco for the same reason that the Insurance Co. was filing the action in this case—to obtain a court order accepting their interpretation of the contract.

Corporations are citizens of the state in which they are incorporated. The Insurance Co. is incorporated in Delaware with its principal place of business in Cincinnati, Ohio. Flanders is an Indiana corporation with its principal place of business in Indiana. The federal District Court had jurisdiction because this was a diversity-of-citizenship case, which is a case filed in federal court by the citizen of one state against a citizen of another state. Pursuant to the United States Constitution, this type of case may be filed in the federal courts, in addition to the possibility of filing the case in the state courts.[37]

4.2 District Court decision (*Cincinnati 1*)

On August 20, 1993, the District Court agreed with the Insurance Co.'s contention and found in its favor. Specifically, the District Court found that "sudden and accidental" is not ambiguous, and "sudden" would be interpreted, under Indiana law, to mean quick, abrupt, or happening without previous notice or with very little notice. The District Court had to apply Indiana law and it concluded that the Indiana courts would view the factual situation in this case as involving a temporal set of circumstances that is not embodied in the term "sudden." Therefore, the discharge at the MEW site would not qualify as sudden and accidental.

Flanders then appealed to the Court of Appeals, which is an intermediate appellate court. It held oral argument on April 12, 1994. This date is significant. On September 2, 1994, while this case was still being considered in the Court of Appeals and a decision had not yet been reached, the Supreme Court of Indiana (Indiana, you will recall, is where Flanders is located) agreed to hear an appeal concerning whether there was insurance coverage in an environmental pollution case involving the interpretation of the "sudden and accidental" clause. Shortly thereafter, Flanders asked the Court of Appeals to delay its decision until the Indiana Supreme Court reached a decision in the case in Indiana interpreting pursuant to Indiana law the relevant clause in the insurance policy.

4.3 Court of Appeals decision (*Cincinnati 1*)

The Court of Appeals denied Flanders' request for a delay of its decision, and, on November 7, 1994, it affirmed the decision of the District Court in favor of the Insurance Co. (*Cincinnati I* decision).[38]

A request for a rehearing of the case was denied by the Court of Appeals on December 13, 1994. The Court of Appeals agreed with the District Court that it should apply Indiana law in deciding the case. The Court of Appeals found that the issue before it was an issue that, as of the date of its decision, had never been ruled upon by the Indiana Supreme Court. According to the Court of Appeals, there was a gap in the law of the State of Indiana. I do not believe that there are gaps in the law, but that is not why I am discussing this case.

Consequently, the Court of Appeals viewed its responsibility in the *Cincinnati* case to be an inquiry into how the Indiana Supreme Court would rule on this issue. The Court of Appeals stated that the issue "raised in this case is straightforward: whether, as a matter of Indiana law, the pollution exclusion clause contained in the three comprehensive general liability policies issued to Flanders by Cincinnati [The Insurance Co.] precludes coverage for liability arising from the gradual environmental contamination at the MEW site."[39] Note that the Court of Appeals characterized the contamination as being a **gradual process**.

The Court of Appeals then declared that the Indiana Supreme Court would decide that the term "sudden" as it is used in the insurance policy is unambiguous and it would be interpreted to exclude coverage for the type of pollution for which Flanders was claiming insurance coverage. The procedure followed by the District Court and the Court of Appeals in applying the law of the state applicable to the case before it (in this case, it would be the law of Indiana where Flanders was located), which is called the Erie Doctrine, was the appropriate procedure. I will discuss the Erie Doctrine in Chapter Six.

Unfortunately, the Court of Appeals was wrong in its prediction of how the Indiana Supreme Court would rule on the issue of the meaning of "sudden and accidental" in this type of insurance policy. Instead of finding that there was no insurance coverage for this type of incident, on March 27, 1996, over a year and a half after the decision of the Court of Appeals in *Cincinnati 1*, the Indiana Supreme Court concluded in the case it was deciding that "sudden and accidental" in the pollution exclusion clause of this type of insurance policy was ambiguous. The Indiana Supreme Court resolved the ambiguity in the insurance policy when it interpreted "sudden and accidental" to mean "unexpected and unintentional."[40] Therefore, Flanders did in fact, under Indiana law, have insurance coverage for the discharge of pollutants at the MEW site.

4.4 District Court decision (*Cincinnati 2*)

Still seeking insurance coverage, Flanders, upon learning of the decision of the Indiana Supreme Court, filed a Motion for Relief from Final Judgment in the District Court. Flanders wanted the District Court to reconsider the case because there now was a definitive interpretation of this type of provision in an insurance contract by the highest court in Indiana. It was now more than eighteen months after Flanders had lost its case in the Court of Appeals. Shortly after Flanders' motion was filed, to further vindicate Flanders' position, the Indiana Supreme Court decided the same issue again in another case. It appeared as though the Indiana Supreme Court was watching the maneuvering in the Flanders case in federal court. The Indiana Supreme Court ruled for the second time that its interpretation of "sudden and accidental" would provide insurance coverage for the type of pollution in the Flanders case.[41] The District Court, however, denied Flanders' motion. Flanders had lost for a second time.

4.5 Court of Appeals decision (*Cincinnati 2*)

The decision we will consider next is the appeal to the Court of Appeals from the District Court decision in *Cincinnati 2*. So, Flanders was in the Court of Appeals for a second time. Flanders was giving the Court of Appeals an opportunity to redeem itself and correct its error in its first decision. The Court of Appeals had misjudged how the Indiana

Supreme Court would rule, but now the Indiana Supreme Court had ruled not once but twice on the very issue Flanders had presented to the Court of Appeals when Flanders was first before the Court of Appeals in *Cincinnati 1*. The Indiana Supreme Court had now definitely clarified the law of Indiana on this issue.

Flanders could point to the Erie Doctrine as requiring that the Court of Appeals find in its favor, since the Indiana Supreme Court had interpreted the "sudden and accidental" provision in a way that Flanders could not be denied insurance coverage. Pursuant to the Erie Doctrine, the Court of Appeals had to apply Indiana law and Indiana law was determinate on this issue. Notwithstanding that argument, Flanders lost for a second time in the Court of Appeals.[42]

Clearly, the Court of Appeals had erred in its first decision when it concluded that the Indiana Supreme Court would interpret the relevant provision in a way that would have resulted in Flanders being denied insurance coverage. I will characterize this decision in *Cincinnati 1* as an incorrect decision by mistake. But, now in the second opportunity to resolve the dispute, the Court of Appeals viewed its decision in the first case as a final decision and it decided that the finality-of-decision doctrine required that a litigant would not be entitled to reopen a federal case that had been closed for more than a year in order to receive the benefit of a decision by the state court which would have been applicable to its case under the Erie Doctrine.[43] The federal courts had not only made the mistake, but they had denied Flanders' request that they not decide the case before the Indiana courts established firm and certain Indiana law on the issue in dispute.

In *Cincinnati 2*, we have a conflict between the principle that the decision should be the same in federal court and in state court (which is the basis for the Erie Doctrine) and the principle (or could it be a policy) of the desirability (or necessity) to achieve finality in litigation. Moreover, this situation involves considering what happens if a rule conflicts with a principle. And, if principles are not part of the law, do they have any place in the judicial process? These issues are beyond the scope of this book, and I will discuss these issues in *The Judge and the Philosopher*. My interest in the *Cincinnati* cases is to highlight the situation when a court makes an incorrect decision by making a mistake.

The Court of Appeals in *Cincinnati 2* decided that the finality-of-decision doctrine was more important than reaching a correct decision by making a decision that would be consistent with the decisions of the Indiana Supreme Court. The decision in *Cincinnati I*, then, is contrary to the Erie Doctrine because the decision in federal court is not consistent with the decision that would have been reached in the Indiana courts. The decision in *Cincinnati 2*, however, is not an incorrect decision because the law, based on the well-established legal rule relating to finality of decisions, was applied. *Cincinnati 2* is, therefore, a correct decision.

It could be argued that the decision of the Court of Appeals in *Cincinnati 1* was a correct decision when it was made, because the Court of Appeals concluded that there was a gap in Indiana law. But can there be a gap, since the Supreme Court in Indiana, according to Indiana law, had to decide the case pending before it one way or the other? Moreover, the trial court in Indiana had decided that Indiana law provided insurance coverage. It was certainly possible, if not likely, that the Supreme Court of Indiana would affirm the decision of the trial court. The trial court's decision was based upon Indiana law. In making its decision, the Indiana Supreme Court applied the same legal rule as the trial court and, in fact, the trial court had accurately anticipated the decision in the Indiana Supreme Court.

What happens if a court reaches an incorrect decision? May an incorrect decision be authorized, authoritative, and binding? Will an incorrect decision be a precedent? If there can be an incorrect decision, can there also be an incorrect law? These questions are not only applicable to cases involving the Erie Doctrine but also relate directly to the situation when a court is considering whether to overrule its own precedent.

The conclusion of the Court of Appeals in *Cincinnati 2* is as follows:

> "We believe that the decision of this Court in *Cincinnati 1* was a valid and well-reasoned effort to carry out our duty under *Erie*. Moreover, the fact that our prediction—and the prediction of the district court—was contrary to the conclusion later reached by the Indiana Supreme Court does not constitute an extraordinary circumstance warranting the reopening of this case to achieve a similar result."[44]

Flanders, then, even though it thought that it had purchased insurance coverage that would pay for any damages caused by its having sent the transformers to MEW in Missouri, would have to pay for its share of the damages from the discharge of pollutants at the MEW site from its own resources. Moreover, this would be the situation even though the courts in the state whose law would be applicable would find that it had insurance coverage. Flanders thought, and had reason to believe, that the law (the applicable law of its state) supported its claim.

Was the decision in *Cincinnati 2* a just decision? Does Flanders have a strong argument when it claims that it has been denied justice because it purchased an insurance policy which the laws of the state in which it is located (Indiana) provided for insurance coverage, but the Court of Appeals in *Cincinnati 1* denied it such coverage? Should the Court of Appeals in *Cincinnati 2* consider whether justice was being granted to the parties before it?

Suppose that the Indiana Supreme Court, in deciding that there was insurance coverage, considered that finding such coverage would provide for a just result. Or suppose that the Indiana Supreme Court decided in favor of the policyholder because it viewed such a result as advantageous for the business environment of Indiana because it would encourage businesses in Indiana to purchase insurance covering pollution if their business might cause pollution. Then, the insurance would provide the funds for remediation of the polluted sites. Should the Court of Appeals have considered these issues in predicting what the Indiana Supreme Court would decide? If it did not and if it believed that there was a gap in Indiana law, what sources should the Court of Appeals have considered in *Cincinnati 1* as those that the Indiana Supreme Court would supposedly consider? If there was a gap in Indiana law, what law would be applied and what would be the source of that law?

The importance of *Cincinnati 1* for our purposes is that this is clearly an incorrect decision. The principle behind the Erie Doctrine is the desirability of ensuring that decisions are the same in the federal court and the state court. Here, the decision in federal court was not at all consistent with Indiana law as declared by the Indiana Supreme Court. Consequently courts may make decisions that are incorrect decisions as a result of mistakes made by the judge (single judge in the District Court and panel of judges in the Court of Appeals). These incorrect decisions will still be binding decisions, binding on the parties, as the Court of Appeals decided in *Cincinnati 2*.

Courts may also reach decisions that are contrary to the pre-existing law that are not the result of the judge having erred. The judge may intentionally decide to change the law in order to arrive at a just and/or wise decision. This may have been a factor in the decisions made by the Indiana courts. If the federal court is predicting what the state courts will decide when they apply Indiana law, should the federal court have considered all the factors that the Indiana courts might consider in making decisions pursuant to Indiana law? These are questions that we will consider when we discuss the Erie Doctrine in Chapter Six.

It is possible, therefore, that the correct decision, even though it is consistent with the pre-existing law, may provide for an unjust result. For example, Flanders would be justified in contending that the decision in *Cincinnati 1* was an unjust decision. The same would be true of the decision in *Cincinnati 2*. All that the Court of Appeals had to do, in fact, is wait for the Indiana Supreme Court to make its decision, and it is not clear why the judges refused Flanders' request that they do so. This then raises the question of whether courts are authorized to use justice as the criterion for making their decisions. This is the subject of our next chapter.

One note of caution before I leave the issue of the incorrect decision. As I will explain in *The Judge and the President* and *The Judge and the Incorrect Decision*, it is not consistent with the way the legal system works to overrule a precedent on the grounds that it is incorrect. A case can be reversed on appeal, however, if the decision of the trial court is incorrect. If the decision is not reversed on appeal, regardless of whether it is correct or incorrect, it becomes part of the pre-existing law for the next case.

The pre-existing law contains many decisions that are incorrect, which I define as a decision that involves the creation of a new legal rule rather than the application of a rule of the pre-existing law. If decisions are overruled on the basis that they were incorrect when they were decided, then the decision that is the result of overruling the precedent can itself be viewed as incorrect and overruled in the next case.

Both the correct decision and the incorrect decision are valid decisions if the judge making the decision had authority to do so and he acted in accordance with the procedures set forth in the law. Do not confuse validity with correctness. An incorrect decision changes the law, but it is still a valid decision.

When we consider *Roe v. Wade* (the decision on abortion) in *The Judge and the Incorrect Decision*, we'll see that it may or may not be a correct decision, but it is nonetheless a valid decision. Since it is a valid decision, it may not be overruled based on whether it is correct or incorrect. It is, just like any other valid decision, part of the pre-existing law.

5.
THE JUST DECISION

It seems odd to be making the argument that justice should be a factor in the judicial decision-making process. If you believe in the traditional theory, or in its twenty-first century variety espoused by Justice Kavanaugh that judges are like umpires, then justice has no place in the judicial process. For those of us who accept the notion that the courts of law are also the courts where justice is dispensed, it is easy to accept that judges, in making their decisions, should consider whether they are making just decisions.

5.1 Facts in *Webb v. McGowin*

Joe Webb was employed by W.T. Smith Lumber Company. He was cleaning the upper floor of the mill on August 3, 1925. It was standard practice when doing so to drop the large blocks of wood from the upper floor to the lower floor by pushing them off the edge of the upper floor to the floor below. On this day, he was pushing a pine block that weighed approximately 75 pounds to the edge of the upper floor.

As Webb started to let the block loose so that it would fall to the lower level, he noticed that J. Greeley McGowin, a co-employee, was walking directly under where the block would fall to the floor below. He was square within the block's fall zone. In other words, McGowin was where the block would fall as Webb was letting it go. If Webb did not alter the path of the block, McGowin would have been severely injured or killed.

The only possible way that Webb could prevent McGowin from being injured was to jump off the edge of the upper floor and change the path of the block by falling to the ground himself, while pushing the block away from McGowin. Webb, alternatively, could have let the block fall. Instead, he opted to save McGowin from being injured. Had Webb failed to hold onto the block and change the trajectory of the block so that the block would not strike McGowin, McGowin would have suffered a very serious injury when the block would hit him.

As a result of jumping with the block and altering its path, Webb suffered serious injuries. His right arm was broken, the heel of his right foot was torn off and his right leg was broken. He was badly crippled for life and unable to do physical or mental labor.

McGowin, on September 1, 1925, in gratitude for saving his life, promised to pay Webb 15 dollars every two weeks for the rest of Webb's life. McGowin did so for more than eight years until he died on January 1, 1934. His estate made two payments and then ceased making additional payments on January 27, 1934. McGowin had failed to include the payments to Webb within his will. Webb filed suit against Floyd McGowin and Joseph McGowin, the executors of J. Greeley McGowin's estate, to enforce the promise to pay him for the rest of his life.

5.2 Decision in *Webb v. McGowin* in the trial court

The trial court found that the promise to make the payments to Webb was not legally binding because contracts which lack consideration are not valid contracts. "Consideration" is a legal term of art, which I will define below. The law, according to the trial court, recognizes a distinction between moral obligations and legal obligations. For a moral obligation to support a subsequent promise to pay, there must have existed a legal or equitable obligation ("equitable" refers to obligations enforced in the equity courts).

But if the promise is just morally binding and not legally binding, it will not be sufficient to create an enforceable contract. An example of the difference between a legally-binding and a morally binding contract can be illustrated by considering a letter of intent. If one enters into a letter of intent to purchase a property, the letter of intent could state that "this letter of intent is not legally binding." The letter of intent would not then create an enforceable contract, even though the letter of intent includes a promise to purchase the property.

The trial court in the Webb case recognized that McGowin did not ask Webb to save his life. Moreover, McGowin had no legal obligation to compensate Webb for doing so. In a sense, McGowin never consented to Webb injuring himself to prevent injury to McGowin. Certainly, McGowin felt a moral obligation and he should have been grateful to Webb for acting as he did. Because of this moral obligation, McGowin made the promise to pay Webb $390 a year for the rest of Webb's life.

Judge Gavin discussed adequacy of consideration in the *O'Brien* case. Generally speaking, as the trial court in Webb recognized, contracts which lack consideration are deemed to be non-enforceable contracts or really not legal contracts. The definition of "consideration" when used in the law is technical. It is defined in the Restatement of Contracts; Section 71 as follows:

1) To constitute consideration, a performance or a return promise must be bargained for,
2) A performance or return promise is bargained for if it is sought by the promisor in exchange for his promise and is given by the promisee in exchange for that promise.
3) The performance may consist of (a) an act other than a promise, or

(b) a forbearance, or (c) the creation, modification or destruction of a legal relation.

4) The performance or return promise may be given to the promisor to some other person. It may be given by the promisee or some other person.

The Restatement is not a statute, and it is not legally binding upon the courts. It is not the law in any single jurisdiction. The Restatement is like a text and may be used by courts as to what the general legal rules might be, as if all the courts in the United States were in one big legal system. It is an alternate source that may be cited as a persuasive source, even though, as I have stated, it is not an authoritative source that carries with it any obligation similar to the obligation of applying the terms of a statute.

The trial court's decision was a correct decision, based upon the common-law legal rule for enforcement of promises. Moral obligations are not legal obligations if there is no legal rule that supports the claim that the promise is legally binding.

5.3 Decision in the appellate court in *Webb v. McGowin*

The Alabama Court of Appeals reversed that decision and held that the contract was enforceable because of the material and substantial benefit that McGowin received. Judge Charles Bricken concluded that McGowin's promise was legally binding and enforceable.[45]

The Court of Appeals was faced with a clear case of a promise being made with no legal consideration for the promise. It is one of the foundational blocks of the common law that a promise without consideration is not a legally binding contract, even though the promise may be morally binding. This is taught in law school in the first-year class on contracts.

Because of the clarity of the pre-existing law, this was not a hard case. H.L.A. Hart describes three types of cases in which judges may create new law in making their decisions. There is a gap in the law—the law contains no rules that apply to the factual situation in the case. The case is within the open texture of the law—the law regarding the factual situation is not clear. The case is not a core case and is, instead, a penumbral case—all language may be vague or ambiguous and the core cases are those in which the factual situation falls clearly within the scope of the legal rule, while, in the penumbral case, the factual situation does not fall clearly within the scope of the legal rule. I will discuss each of these concepts in more detail in *The Judge and the Philosopher*.

In the *Webb* case, the pre-existing law was absolutely clear and there was no doubt that the correct decision would be to find against Webb. The Court of Appeals, however, reversed the decision of the trial court and found that Webb was entitled to continuation of the payments until his death.

I do not believe that Judge Bricken's decision for Webb in the Court of Appeals reflected his personal bias against McGowin. Relief was not granted to Webb because he was Irish, or white, or redheaded or named Webb. The question of a legal remedy for Webb does not involve the judge's personal prejudice in making his decision. Judge Bricken found for Webb because a denial of a remedy for him would have been unjust.

This case presents a conflict between the desirability of a correct decision versus the desirability of a just decision. The Court of Appeals decision is an example of the element of justice prevailing over the element of correctness. The correct decision has been sacrificed for the just decision. It is typical of just decisions that the judge looks carefully at the facts, considers seriously the effect of the decision on the parties and frames the decision narrowly by creating a narrow rule or a small exception to the otherwise applicable legal rule of the pre-existing law.

Judge Gavin in the *O'Brien* case also looked carefully at the facts and considered the effect of his decision on the parties. He opted not to reach the just decision, even though he did consider the morality and ethics of his decision. He decided to reach the correct decision.

5.4 Concurring opinion in the *Webb* case

It is interesting to note that Judge Sanford of the Alabama Court of Appeals filed a concurring opinion in *Webb v. McGowin*. Appellate courts generally sit as a panel of judges, usually three of them. If one of the judges agrees with the result being reached but does not agree with the reason for the decision, he may file a concurring opinion, which is what Judge Sanford did. He did not agree with Judge Bricken's reasoning, but he did quote Chief Justice John Marshall, an eminent justice of the United States Supreme Court: "I do not think that law ought to be separated from justice, where it is at most doubtful."

5.5 The legal rule created in the *Webb* case

The narrowness of the *ratio decidendi* (the legal rule to be derived from the decision) of the *Webb* case can be determined by considering both the language of the opinion and the references to the decision in later cases. It is a fact of legal history that the *Webb* case has not had any appreciable effect in endangering the general understanding of the legal rules concerning contracts and the enforcement of contracts which are made for a valid consideration. It is still good law that contracts for which there is no valid consideration will not be legally binding. Therefore, it is fair to conclude that the legal rule established in the *Webb* case is a very narrow one.

The *Webb* case is a precedent that would, in my opinion, be applicable only to cases in which the promisee suffered a serious debilitating injury in conferring a benefit to the promisor who received some actual material benefit as a direct result of the act of the promisee. In addition, the promisor must make a credible promise because he feels morally obligated to compensate the person to whom he is grateful (in this case, for the promisee's sacrifice).

It would appear to be essential according to the holding in the *Webb* case that the promisor is acknowledging a moral obligation when he makes the specific promise to the person who suffered harm in order to grant to him the benefit. The holding in the decision is the reason for the legal rule created in the decision. In other words, the holding establishes its precedential value.

Moreover, the promise must be unambiguous. Perhaps, if it is an oral promise, it also must be acted upon for a period of time to establish credibility. When the legal rule to be derived from the decision in the *Webb* case is described in these narrow terms, there is no serious threat to the general legal rule that consideration is required in order to have a valid contract.

The Restatement of Contracts included Section 86 after the decision in the *Webb* case to clarify which moral obligations will be legally enforceable:

1) A promise made in recognition of a benefit previously received by the promisor from the promisee is binding to the extent necessary to prevent **injustice**.
2) A promise is not binding under subsection (1): (a) if the promisee conferred the benefit as a gift or for other reasons the promisor has not been **unjustly** enriched or (b) to the extent that its value is disproportionate to the benefit."[46] (Emphases mine).

The reader should note that the authors of *The Restatement of Contracts* have placed, in my terminology, the concept of the just decision into their version of the legal rule for enforcement of moral obligations. The reference to the value being disproportionate to the benefit is similar to the inadequacy of consideration issue raised in the *O'Brien* case. I do not believe that there is any similar obligation of reaching just decisions imposed upon umpires in the *Official Rules of Baseball.*

5.6 Some additional cases involving the just decision

Many cases in which justice is a factor involve the allocation of burdens, such as which party should sustain the loss. *Lloyd v. Grace, Smith & Co,* is such a case. The plaintiff suffered a loss when she was defrauded by an employee of the defendant. The defendant claimed that the employee did not have the authority to act on behalf of the company. The judge in the case was Baron Edward Macnaghten, who was an Anglo-Irish barrister, a member of the House of Commons and a law lord in the House of Lords.

Lord Macnaghten explicitly considered the suitability of his decision as it affected the parties before the court:

> "So much for the case as it stands upon the authorities. But putting aside the authorities altogether, I must say that it would be absolutely shocking to my mind if Mr. Smith were not held liable for the fraud of his agent in the present case. When Mrs. Lloyd put herself in the hands of the firm how was she to know what the exact position of Sandles was? Mr. Smith carries on business under a style or firm which implies that unnamed persons are, or may be, included in its members. Sandles speaks and acts as if he were one of the firm. He points to the deed boxes in the room and tells her that her deeds are quite safe in 'our' hands. Naturally enough she signs the documents he puts before her without trying to understand what they were. Who is to suffer for this man's fraud? The person who relied on Mr. Smith's accredited representative, or Mr. Smith, who put this rogue in his own place and clothed him with his own authority?"[47]

Needless to mention, Mr. Smith lost the case.

In the *Lloyd* case, Baron Macnaghten declares that the kind of case before him was not considered when the applicable legal rule was established. The difficulty of fitting specific factual situations into rules that are framed in general terms is a common theme in cases in which the just decision is considered.

In *Wilder Grain Co. v. Falker*, the plaintiff sought compensation from the administrator of an estate for grain he had supplied the estate in order to preserve livestock belonging to it. The grain was supplied after the death of the testator (the person who had died and left a valid will), but the administrator of the estate had not ordered it. The grain had been delivered prior to the date on which the administrator was appointed.

The court held that the plaintiff could look to the estate for payment for the grain. Consider the reasoning of the court:

> "Broad considerations of justice favor a plaintiff who has thus not only performed an act of mercy but who has also saved for the estate assets which would otherwise have been lost. It would not be fair and just that creditors who have themselves done nothing should profit at his expense."[48]

The court candidly admitted that it was not applying the pre-existing law because the instant case was an exceptional case: "It seems evident that the court in these cases and in several others . . . in stating general rules, did not have in mind an exceptional case like this."[49] There can be no doubt that the court in this case realized that the general rules declared in the previous cases clearly included the instant case within the scope of the language of the rules. The court opted, instead of applying the rules of the pre-existing law, not to make a correct decision but to make a just decision.

In *Hutson v. Hutson*, the plaintiff "married" a woman who was still married to someone else, though the plaintiff did not know this. He conveyed (transferred) a parcel of land to a third party who conveyed the property to the plaintiff and his "wife" as tenants by the entireties (this is a form of ownership for a married couple in which the survivor of the married couple becomes the sole owner of the property when one member of the married couple dies). The marriage was annulled, and the plaintiff sued to have the deed rescinded (cancelled). The court rescinded the deed declaring that any other decision would be a great injustice to the plaintiff.[50]

In another case involving fraud, *Liebman v. Rosenthal*, the applicable general rule was that the court would not grant relief to a litigant involved in an illegal contract because the parties are *in pari delicto* (the parties are jointly committing an illegal act). The event occurred, however, in a wartime context. During World War II, the plaintiff sought visas for himself and his family allowing them to leave France in order to avoid the Germans who were occupying France. The plaintiff contracted with the defendant to obtain these visas. The plaintiff gave the defendant jewelry to be used to bribe the Portuguese consul to grant the visas. The defendant failed to perform the contract and he did not return the jewelry.

After the war, the plaintiff found the defendant in New York and sued him for the value of the jewelry. Because of the extreme pressure on the plaintiff to save himself and his family, the court held that the parties were not *in pari delicto*, and the court found for the plaintiff.[51] Parties according to the general legal rule are acting *in pari delicto* when they are co-conspirators in committing a criminal act.

I could cite many other examples of courts reaching just decisions, even though such decisions were inconsistent with pre-existing law. In many of these cases, the court is creating an exception to a general rule in order to achieve a just result. The problem usually is not one of lack of clarity of the general rule. It is not a gap in the law nor a penumbral case because the factual situation fits within the scope and the terms of the general rule. These are situations where the court decides to reach a just result, notwithstanding the otherwise applicable legal rule.

Judge Jerome N. Frank and the just decision

Jerome N. Frank, one of the most prominent and influential of the American Legal Realists, was a judge on the federal Court of Appeals. Before becoming a judge (and continuing after he was a judge), he was a legal philosopher. I will discuss his legal philosophy in more detail in *The Judge and the Philosopher*.

Frank contends that judges decide cases by intuition (which legal theorists often refer to as a "hunch") to reach decisions that are "fair and just or wise or expedient."[52] Frank, in this statement, is referring to what judges actually do; his contention is that the judicial decision is a result of the judge's "intuition of fitness of solution to the problem."

I do not intend to discuss Frank's views on the psychology of how judges think. I am primarily interested in the procedure by which judges justify their decisions (as determined by studying their oral and written statements, especially those in their judicial opinions). Even if intuition, or a hunch, is a factor in judicial thinking, the thought process would be within the context of applying legal rules and performing judicial duties.

In later versions of Frank's philosophy, the emphasis is not upon the psychology of the judge but is about the judge's desire to reach a just decision. If this just decision would conflict with the correct decision, Frank maintains that the judge should render the just decision. He expands upon this contention by declaring that what judges actually do is reach a just decision and then justify it by reciting legal rules that will lead to this just decision.

Frank's theory of a desirable judicial procedure for deciding cases is as follows:

"*The judge, at his best, is an arbitrator*, a 'sound man' who strives to do justice to the parties by exercising a wise discretion with reference to the peculiar circumstances of the case. He does not merely 'find' or invent some generalized rule which he 'applies' to the facts presented to him. He does 'equity' in the sense in which Aristotle—when thinking most clearly—described it."[53] (Frank's italics).

According to Frank, equity consists of "fairness, tolerance, mercy, the spirit of kindliness."[54]

He recommends that judges become more aware of the justice or injustice of their decisions in individual cases. Justice requires, according to Frank, adjusting the rules of pre-existing law so that just results are obtained in individual cases.[55] To achieve justice in making judicial decisions, he argues that "more adequate consideration of the specific facts of specific cases" is necessary.[56]

Frank bases the contention that judges should be concerned with the justice of their decisions on three factors: (1) the settlement of disputes is the central and most important aspect of the judicial decision; (2) there is in reality much less reliance on the pre-existing law than is normally supposed; and (3) the difficulty of anticipating future needs is so great that judges should be more concerned with fair solutions in cases before them than with attempting to devise wise rules for a future they may only hazily portend.

The first reason Frank gives is that the predominant responsibility of judges is the orderly settlement of individual cases rather than concern for whether their decisions will be in accord with the pre-existing law or consideration of the formulation of wise rules of law for the future.[57] Probably no one will dispute that courts exist to settle controversies presented to them. It would seem naturally to follow from this that judges in settling controversies should, in so far as it is possible, attempt to render a just decision rather than an unjust one. This view of the judge's responsibility is buttressed by the common-law rule that the court should not decide hypothetical cases, but judges should only decide real controversies presented to the court.

The second argument that Frank employs is the assertion that there is in reality less reliance on the pre-existing law than is commonly thought. By reliance, he is referring to those instances where people arrange their affairs after having received legal advice about the procedure by which they can achieve some desired legal result. Frank would go still further and inquire whether the litigant in the case where a pre-existing legal rule is going to be applied (or not applied) has himself relied upon his lawyer's understanding of the applicable legal rules prior to initiating some action.[58] It is interesting to speculate whether Judge Gavin would have taken a different position if both parties in the *O'Brien* case had consulted lawyers before the non-compete agreement was signed.

This focus on the litigants, however, ignores the interests of people not parties before the court who have nevertheless relied on the law. These persons may have looked to the law and conducted their affairs in order to achieve a desired legal effect and an adverse change in the law will, of course, result in the non-fulfillment of their expectations. The decision made by the judge, while it may be a just result for the parties, may become a precedent that will affect future cases. Because of reliance upon the pre-existing law, the courts should hesitate to alter the law upon which members of the society have relied. Certainty in the law is essential for order within the society.

The third argument is that the future is so unpredictable that the judge should be more concerned with achieving a just result in the instant case than with establishing a rule that will fairly determine future cases that may never arise.[59] The revised rule may be unjust in future cases because of a change in the society or a miscalculation of future conditions. But legal rules are necessary to guide persons in planning their activities. The law is necessary to control behavior either by conscious consideration of the law before acting or by the law seeping into the public consciousness and creating folkways or patterns of behavior which in turn govern social conduct. Legal rules are not solely makeweights to be juggled by judges to justify their decisions; they also comprise the law that governs behavior.

In many cases, the consideration of a just decision will be insignificant because no important question of justice will be involved. For example, there are statements in the law reports containing opinions written by judges in deciding cases such as the following:

> "What is needed here is a clear guide which will tell the parties where they may sue in federal court and where they may not. There are no political, economic, sociological or ethical considerations involved that we can see. The question is not unlike that of the rules of the road for traffic. It can travel on the right, or it can travel on the left, but a car driver must know which side he is to take. And so here."[60]

In those cases, the cases in which the most relevant goal is the firm establishment of a definite legal rule, the courts should concern themselves primarily with correct decisions and establishing rules that work effectively and efficiently. The possibility of an unjust result in these cases is of small significance.

Furthermore, in all cases, assuming that judges in the past have tried to reach just decisions, there is at least a presumption in favor of following those decisions because those decisions indicate what the just result in the case would be. The opinion of a single individual is always subject to limitations of individual ability and the law has built up within its rules over the years a conception of which decisions will be just decisions. In other words, to a certain extent, the legal rules are a guide as to what the just decision would be.

Frank is not alone in mentioning that there are factors like justice that should be considered by judges in reaching what I am calling the just decision. Sir Carleton Kemp Allen, a professor and warden of Rhodes House at the University of Oxford, discusses mercy,[61] and Rudolf Stammler, a professor of law at several German universities, speaks of grace.[62] Roscoe Pound, Dean of Harvard Law School, mentions individualization,[63] the administrative element,[64] and equitable application.[65]

After he became a judge, Frank, specifically and obviously, tried to place great stress on the just result in the individual case, which is consistent with his legal philosophy. As a judge, Frank also, contrary to his legal philosophy, explicitly recognized the obligation of a judge to apply the preexisting law.[66] He also came to recognize the importance of the correct decision. In fact, after becoming a judge, he may have also changed his views as a legal philosopher.

J. Mitchell Rosenberg, the author of *Jerome Frank: Jurist and Philosopher*, points out that Frank, in the Preface to the 6th edition of his most popular book, *Law and the Modern Mind*, declares that "the rules are significant."[67] This statement was made after Frank had served seven years as an appellate judge. In *Courts on Trial*, one-half year later, Frank states that "no sensible person suggests that *stare decisis* be abandoned."[68] Robert Jerome Glennon, author of another book about Frank called *The Iconoclast as Reformer: Jerome Frank's Impact on American Law*, noted that Frank, as a judge, "wrote lengthy opinions, fine-tuned legal rules, quarreled over the scope and intended meaning of prior judicial decisions and adumbrated policy considerations to govern present and future cases."[69]

According to Rosenberg, Frank came to recognize the goals of certainty, uniformity, continuity and stability as important for the legal system.[70] Glennon has a slightly different view, and he states that "Frank elaborated important themes from his legal philosophy in his judicial opinions. As a judge, he remained concerned with 'doing justice,' frequently disregarded *stare decisis*, and bent legal rules to achieve desirable results."[71]

In summary, Rosenberg and Glennon seem to agree that Frank, as a judge, looked to precedents to decide most of the cases, occasionally applied the rule in the precedent but suggested that the Supreme Court might consider overruling the precedent, and occasionally wrote a dissenting opinion to increase the possibility that the Supreme Court would accept a case. Dissenting opinions are written by judges who disagree with the result that the majority of the court prefers. Frank was more likely in civil cases to write concurring opinions and, in criminal cases, dissenting opinions.[72]

Most significantly, even though Frank very much disagreed with the death penalty, he accepted Supreme Court precedent that appellate courts do not modify trial court sentences. As an appellate judge, Frank affirmed trial court sentences of execution.

5.8 Describing the just decision

My definition of the just decision is that a just decision is a fair, suitable and right (in the moral sense) solution to the issue before the court taking into consideration all the claims of the parties in a civil case and all the interests of the defendant, the victims and the prosecution in a criminal case. In most cases, in the usual cases, a correct decision will be a just decision. But, in some exceptional cases, the correct decision will be an unjust decision. The element of justice forces us to consider in each particular case whether that case is exceptional, extraordinary or unusual.

Sir Carleton Kemp Allen explicitly recognizes the importance of justice as a consideration in reaching judicial decisions:

"We speak of the judge's function as the 'administration of justice,' and we are sometimes apt to forget that we mean, or ought to mean, exactly what we say. Popular catchwords are too fond of distinguishing between the administration of law and the administration of justice, as if they were two different things. Nobody claims that the law always achieves ideal moral justice, but whatever the inevitable technicalities of legal science may be, they exist for the preservation of one aim only, which is also the aim of the judge's office: to do justice between litigants."[73]

The relative weight of the element of justice in the reaching of judicial decisions will differ in various types of cases in different areas of the law.

It presents a false picture to assume that the judge can consider the factual situation in isolation and independent of other factors in making the just decision. The judge is not able to place his knowledge of the law in a separate compartment of his mind. The judge sees the facts in the light of his legal training and his framing of the issues is pre-determined by his knowledge of the legal rules. The issues presented to him will be characterized by the pre-existing legal categories of various areas of the law. He will be influenced by the reasoning of eminent judges in prior cases. He will be familiar with the legal principles that are the underpinning of the legal rules. The judge's whole outlook is within this legal context.

The judge also cannot ignore that adherence to pre-existing law is always necessary so that the law will be certain and will satisfy reasonable expectations of how it will be applied. In short, certainty of the law is of great importance. For the legal counselor, certainty is necessary to allow for predictability so that she may advise her clients accordingly. The law also must be certain for the citizens to be able to obey the law and to understand what the law expects of them.

The other argument for emphasis on the correct decision when considering the just decision is based upon the reality that the concept of justice is fraught with difficulties and uncertainties, and one must continually be hesitant about whether one really knows what the just result will be. Roscoe Pound, the Dean of Harvard Law School, makes this point in his discussion of the classic case of the tailor who in good faith makes a suit of clothes for one customer out of cloth belonging to someone else and the court must then determine who is the owner of the suit.[74] There is no solution to this case that is wholly satisfactory to all concerned, which illustrates the elusiveness of the just decision.

Justice Louis Brandeis, who is one of the greatest judges in American judicial history, recognizes this difficulty: "*Stare decisis* is usually the wise policy, because in most matters it is more important that the applicable rule of law be settled than that it be settled right."[75] But, once again, we cannot ignore that applying settled rules may result in unacceptable decisions. Consideration of the just decision allows for avoiding unjust results.

Justice is a difficult concept to explain. Many philosophers agree that all persons have a natural sense of what is just, and, even more so, of what is unjust. These philosophers describe many different aspects of justice. While justice is not easily defined, everyone has a view as to what it means.

Consider the following questions:

As between O'Brien, who wanted to pursue his occupation, and Desco, which invested in training him, which party should suffer the loss?

As between Flanders, which purchased insurance coverage for the cost of remediation that is the result of environmental pollution, and Cincinnati Insurance Co., which issued insurance coverage for environmental pollution that was "sudden and accidental," which party should suffer the loss?

As between Webb, who was incapacitated in saving McGowin's life, and McGowin's heirs who will inherit his estate, which party should suffer the loss?

As between Lloyd, who trusted the employee of Grace, Smith & Co., whose employee defrauded her when she came to their office, which party should suffer the loss?

As between Wilder Grain Co., which delivered the grain to save Falker's livestock, and Falker's Estate, which did not specifically request that the grain be delivered after Falker had died, which party should suffer the loss?

As between Hutson, who transferred the property to the woman he thought that he had married, and Hutson's "wife" who was still married to someone else, which party should suffer the loss?

As between Liebman, who gave the necklace to Rosenthal to use in bribing the Portuguese consul, and Rosenthal who did not obtain the visas for Liebman, which party should suffer the loss?

In each of these seven cases, you may determine which party has the stronger argument for justice requiring a judgment in their favor. After you make that decision, you must compare that potential just decision with the value of a correct decision and decide which is more important. Then, you must consider that this decision will be a precedent and that the legal rule you apply will control the outcome in cases that will be decided after this decision. The issue of the consequences of this decision will be the subject of our next three chapters.

Our next three chapters consider the wise decision. As distinct from the correct decision that is consistent with the pre-existing law, the just decision and the wise decision are two types of alternate source decisions. While there are other possible alternate sources than justice and wisdom, I have found that justice and wisdom, when combined with the correct decision, provide a well-balanced format for evaluating judicial decisions. The correct decision allows us to consider the past— the decisions made over the years and the basis for such decisions. The just decision focusses on the present—the impact of the decision on the parties in the courtroom. The wise decision looks to the future— the consequences of the decision being made. Also, it is important to remember that the correct decision may also be the just decision and/or the wise decision.

I will return to Justice Brandeis for my first example of a wise decision. This is a decision which is also not a correct decision since it not only does not apply pre-existing law, but it overrules a settled precedent that was law for almost 100 years and the decision wiped out of judicial history thousands of decisions that were made based upon the settled precedent.

6.
THE WISE DECISION

I have selected *Erie Railroad Co. v. Tompkins* as a good example of the wise decision. It is a case in which a court (in this case, the U.S. Supreme Court) considered the source of law to be applied in diversity-of-citizenship cases in federal court. The reader will recall that the District Court and the Court of Appeals in Chapter Four in the *Cincinnati* cases (the cases involving environmental pollution and the insurance policy) had to apply Indiana law to decide the case. The federal court had to apply state law in the diversity-of-citizenship case, rather than federal law, because of the decision in *Erie Railroad Co. v. Tompkins.*

6.1 Background of the Erie Doctrine
The Erie Doctrine prescribes which body of law the courts in the federal judicial system (the various federal District Courts, Courts of Appeals and Supreme Court) should apply in a diversity-of-citizenship case. Diversity-of-citizenship cases can involve a large variety of subjects. These cases may be filed in federal court because the United States Constitution provides for jurisdiction in federal court when a

citizen of one state is suing a citizen of another state. The plaintiff, the party who initiates the case, may elect to file it in federal court rather than in state court or the defendant, the party being sued, may opt to move the case from the state court to the federal court if the parties are citizens of different states.[76]

If a case is filed in state court, in general, the law of the state hearing the case would be the relevant law to be applied (the "applicable law"). The law of the state in which the trial is being held, however, may require that the court look to the law of another state or some other jurisdiction in deciding the case. If it did so, it would be because the law of the jurisdiction in which the case was being tried requires that another jurisdiction's laws be utilized to decide the case. An example could be the law of the state where an automobile accident occurred.[77]

When applying the law of another jurisdiction as the applicable law to be used to decide the case (sometimes referred to as a conflict-of-laws case). the decision is authorized and binding. The decision, however, is not authoritative in the sense that it does not result in a precedent for the jurisdiction where the trial is being conducted. The court applying the law of another jurisdiction also does not, in theory and generally in practice, change the applicable law, the law of the jurisdiction whose law is being applied.

In short, the responsibility of the court applying the law of another jurisdiction is solely that of reaching a correct decision (a decision consistent with the pre-existing law of the jurisdiction whose law is the appliable law). Each state in the United States has its own legal system and its own hierarchy of legal rules. In fact, prior to the states becoming states, when they were the American colonies, each colony had its own legal system. Each of the original thirteen colonies loosely adopted the English common law.[78]

In England, the common law has been developed over centuries by a succession of judicial decisions. While the English common law was applied in general in the colonies, the courts in the various colonies adopted only portions of the English common law. The courts in each colony selected which legal rules they thought were appropriate for the conditions in their colony.

So, unlike England where there is a coherent set of rules applied in the entire country, each colony adopted its own version of the common law. Therefore, instead of there being one common law in all the colonies, there were multiple common laws, with each colony and later each state having its own set of legal rules applicable in that colony or state. Therefore, each state has its own legal system and there is no common, uniform legal system in all the states.

6.2 *Swift v. Tyson*

Swift v. Tyson is a case involving a negotiable instrument like a promissory note (which was called a "bill of exchange" in 1836 when the transaction occurred). The bill of exchange was for the sum of $1,540.30. The debtors on the bill of exchange, Nathaniel Norton and Jainus S. Keith, did not pay the debt when it became due. John Swift, the plaintiff, had accepted the bill from George W. Tyson, the defendant. When the debt was not paid, Swift sued Tyson in the federal district court in New York.

Tyson had accepted the bill of exchange from Norton and Keith. Tyson claimed that he had been defrauded by Norton and Keith and, therefore, his agreement to pay the debt of the bill of exchange he gave Swift was not legally enforceable. At the trial, Swift put the bill of exchange in evidence. Tyson wanted to introduce evidence of the fraud, to which Swift objected. Tyson claimed there was a failure of consideration in his transaction with Norton and Keith. Swift had accepted the bill with no knowledge of the Tyson/Norton and Keith transaction.

The trial judge was uncertain about how he should decide the issue of whether Tyson could raise the defense he wanted to assert in order to challenge the validity of the bill of exchange. The law was different in New York where the trial was being held in comparison to some of the other states. The trial court certified the case to the United States Supreme Court to resolve the issue. Justice Joseph Story wrote the opinion for the Supreme Court.

When the United States was formed, one of the early acts of the Congress was to adopt the Judiciary Act of 1789.[79] Section 34 of Chapter 20 of the Judiciary Act of 1789 provides "that the laws of the several states, except where the Constitution, treaties, or statutes of the United States shall otherwise require or provide, shall be regarded as rules of decision in trials at common law in the Courts of the United States, in cases where they apply."[80]

The issue that the Supreme Court had to decide was what was included in the term "the laws" in the Judiciary Act. The Supreme Court ruled that "the laws" would include statutes and local customs having the force of law but would not include decisions of the state courts. The Supreme Court's reasoning was as follows:

> "They [decisions of state courts] are, at most, only evidence of what the laws are, and are not of themselves laws. They are often re-examined, reversed and qualified by the Courts themselves, whenever they are found to be defective, or ill-founded, or otherwise incorrect."[81]

Note the reference to the possibility of an incorrect decision, though I would limit its use to the reversal of a prior decision and not to the overruling of a prior decision. It is not clear that Justice Story would agree.

Therefore, the federal courts were instructed by the Supreme Court to apply in diversity-of-citizenship cases general law, to wit, a federal common law to be developed by the federal courts. Justice Story wanted to make the commercial law consistent throughout the country. He wanted national legal rules to govern commercial cases.

It should be obvious that the Supreme Court is acknowledging in *Swift v. Tyson* that federal judges will be creating, examining, reversing and qualifying the legal rules that will be found in precedents of cases decided by federal judges when deciding cases pending before them. They will not be merely calling balls or strikes and this was an obvious feature of the opinion written in 1842. The federal common law had to be created.

Therefore, according to the Supreme Court in the *Swift* case, the common law included an English precedent that held that negotiable instruments should be governed by the laws of the commercial world and not the laws of a single country.[82] Accordingly, accepting the same reasoning, the legal rule applied by the Supreme Court for negotiable instruments in the United States was to accept general commercial law and not the law of a particular jurisdiction. Applying general commercial law, a debt that existed before a negotiable instrument was signed could constitute consideration for the negotiable instrument. The Supreme Court cited several English cases and a decision by the Supreme Court of Connecticut (it made no difference, therefore, that the federal court which heard the case was sitting in New York rather than Connecticut).[83]

The Supreme Court acknowledged that local court decisions on general commercial law are entitled to consideration and respect. The laws of New York as formulated by the courts of New York would not be applied, however, to decide the case. Instead, the Supreme Court required the federal courts to develop their own version of the commercial law to be applied in resolving diversity-of-citizenship cases.

In *Swift*, apparently, the Supreme Court wanted to ensure that the credit and circulation of commercial paper would be facilitated. Persons who accept commercial paper should be able to rely upon general rules established in federal commercial law and should not be concerned about local rules in a particular state that they might find it difficult to ascertain. The Supreme Court was motivated by the desire to promote commerce, which was regarded as a beneficial social policy.[84]

The reader will recall in the discussion of the *Webb* case that the common law recognized that a pre-existing debt may constitute valid consideration for a contract. In the *Webb* case, there was no pre-existing debt. In the *Swift* case, there was an underlying debt that Tyson owed to Swift, so that the underlying debt was the consideration for the contract, which led to the conclusion that the contract was a valid contract. Hence, Swift could collect on the bill from Tyson.

The Supreme Court was motivated by the desire to achieve consistency among the federal courts. Consistency was not the result, however, because the federal common law that the federal courts developed was different than the common law of the various states, so there was now consistency among the federal courts but inconsistency between the federal courts and the state courts.

The legal rule established by the Supreme Court in 1842 in *Swift v. Tyson* requiring federal courts to apply federal common law in diversity-of-citizenship cases when there was no applicable state legislation or custom was the prevailing view until the Supreme Court considered the same question in 1938 in *Erie Railroad Co. v. Tompkins*, almost 100 years later. In the *Erie* case, the Supreme Court overruled its long-standing precedent established by its decision in *Swift v. Tyson* and created the Erie Doctrine.[85]

6.3 Black and White Taxicab & Transfer Co. v. Brown & Yellow Taxicab & Transfer Co.

Before I discuss the *Erie* case, I want to mention the one case in addition to *Swift v. Tyson* that the Supreme Court mentioned in the majority opinion in the *Erie* case. The Supreme Court has nine justices, and the majority opinion would be the opinion written by a single justice in which at least four other justices join. During the years between *Swift v. Tyson* and *Erie Railroad Co. v. Tompkins*, there was only one decision that was relevant to the dramatic change to be made in creating the Erie Doctrine that the Supreme Court in *Erie* regarded as influential. It was not, however, the decision in this case that was significant, but the dissenting opinion. The importance of dissenting opinions is not that they create legal rules. It is that they forecast potential changes in the legal rules, and they may be a persuasive factor in making the change.

The case mentioned in the *Erie* case is *Black & White Taxicab & Transfer Co. v. Brown & Yellow Taxicab & Transfer Co.*[86] Brown & Yellow was a company in Bowling Green, Kentucky. In 1921, it had an exclusive franchise from the Louisville & Nashville Railroad to park cabs and solicit customers at its passenger railroad station. Black & White wanted to compete for those customers.

Under Kentucky law, Black & White had the right to compete for the customers. Black & White was a Kentucky corporation. Brown & Yellow, which was a Kentucky corporation, terminated that corporation and reconstituted itself as a Tennessee corporation. It did so in order to establish diversity-of-citizenship. Brown & Yellow then entered into a contract with the railroad for the exclusive taxi rights. It, in effect, manufactured diversity of citizenship in order to qualify for diversity jurisdiction. Brown & Yellow wanted the federal common law to be applied rather than Kentucky law.

This went beyond forum-shopping (for example, "forum shopping" is the litigation practice of plaintiffs suing in federal court rather than in state court in order to avoid the application of the common law of the state). Brown & Yellow had laid the groundwork for creating jurisdiction in the federal court. Brown & Yellow exploited the system by creating diversity of citizenship in order to qualify for jurisdiction in the federal courts. It selected which body of law it wanted to have applied to its case.

In an additional step to avoid Kentucky law because its contract would be void under Kentucky law, Brown & Yellow entered into the contract with the railroad in Tennessee. It then filed its lawsuit against Black & White and the railroad in the federal court (the railroad was later dropped out of the case).

The contract between Brown & Yellow and the railroad was legal according to federal common law and in virtually all the states except for Kentucky, Indiana and Mississippi. The majority opinion in the Supreme Court found that "[t]he cases cited show that the decisions of the Kentucky Court of Appeals holding such arrangements [like the contract between Brown & Yellow and the railroad] invalid are contrary to the common law."[87] Brown & Yellow was successful in convincing the Supreme Court in accordance with its decision in *Swift v. Tyson* to apply federal common law rather than the law of Kentucky (where the railroad station was located).

Black & White did not argue that the Supreme Court should deviate from the rule established in *Swift v. Tyson* that required the federal courts to apply federal common law in diversity-of-citizenship cases rather than the common law of the relevant state (which would have otherwise been Kentucky where the railroad station was located). This case is significant because Justice Oliver Wendell Holmes, Jr., one of the greatest justices to have served on the Supreme Court, filed a dissenting opinion in which Justices Brandeis and Stone joined.

Justice Holmes did not suggest that the Supreme Court should overrule *Swift v. Tyson*. When a case is overruled, it loses its status as a precedent. Instead, he wanted to create an exception to applying federal common law in a case involving real property rights. Justice Holmes wanted to apply local law (Kentucky law) because the land upon which the railroad station was located was in Kentucky.[88] The most important point that he stressed is that there really was no general common law for the federal courts to apply.

Law exists, according to Justice Holmes, only if there is some definite authority behind it. Each state is a separate jurisdiction, and each state has its own common law. There is no general common law for the federal courts to discover and apply to decide cases.[89] Before this dissenting opinion and the decision in the *Erie* case, no one questioned whether there was a federal common law and cases decided before *Erie* that were based upon federal common law were regarded as having been correctly decided.

6.4 Factual situation in *Erie Railroad Co. v. Tompkins*

Harry Tompkins, a Pennsylvania citizen and resident, was injured by Erie Railroad Company's train. The accident occurred about 2:30 a.m. on July 27, 1934, while he was walking in Hughestown, Pennsylvania. He was walking on a commonly used footpath which was adjacent to the railroad tracks of the Erie Railroad's Erie and Wyoming Valley Railroad. A friend of Tompkins had driven him to where Rock Street crossed the railroad tracks. This was one block from Hughes Street on which his house was located (Hughes Street is a stub-end street which terminates at the railroad tracks).

Tompkins was walking home on a path next to the railroad tracks. He had walked on this path many times. The path was parallel to the tracks, and he had to walk about 115 feet to reach Hughes Street. The path was approximately two feet wide and approximately two feet from the end of the railroad ties which supported the tracks, though it was less wide in some places. The locomotive extended one foot wider than the end of the ties and the railroad cars were another five inches wider than the locomotive. Tompkins could have walked on a cartway for vehicles adjacent to and parallel to the footpath that he was on.

He knew that railroad cars travelled on these tracks and that the trains had whistles and headlights. It was a dark night with no artificial light (except for the light on the train). The train was going in the same direction as Tompkins. He heard the whistle of the train as it crossed Rock Street. After the locomotive passed him, he saw a black object protruding from a railroad car. It looked to him like it was an open door on a refrigerator car.

There was time and space for Tompkins. to step aside, but he did not do so. He stayed on the path next to the tracks. He was hit by the object swinging from the side of the train as the train passed him. Before he could have even raised his hands, he was struck on his head and thrown to the ground. His right arm was crushed by the wheels of the train.

There was no Pennsylvania statute related to this factual situation. Pennsylvania common law regarded Tompkins as a trespasser. Pennsylvania law distinguished persons crossing the tracks, who would not be regarded as a trespasser, from someone walking parallel to the tracks. He could recover under Pennsylvania law only if he could establish that the railroad had acted in a wanton or willful manner (gross negligence) and was not merely negligent (ordinary negligence).

Neither the federal District Court nor the Court of Appeals in the *Erie* case, however, applied Pennsylvania law. After all, the established law for diversity-of-citizenship cases for almost 100 years provided that federal common law should be applied rather than the law of the state in which the accident occurred. The federal common law required only ordinary negligence to establish liability in a case in which the railroad owed a duty of care to persons walking along railroad tracks on a commonly used path.

6.5 Decision in the *Erie* case in District Court

Tompkins filed suit in the United States District Court for the Southern District of New York rather than in the state court. If he had filed in Pennsylvania state court, he would not have won the case. If he had filed in New York state court, New York conflict-of-law rules would have required the New York court to apply Pennsylvania law because the accident occurred in Pennsylvania, and he would have lost there. There was diversity of citizenship because Tompkins was a citizen and resident of Pennsylvania and Erie Railroad Co., which owned and operated the railroad, was incorporated in New York and was, therefore, a New York corporation.

Since Tompkins was on a commonly used pathway when he was injured, he claimed that he was entitled to prevail if he could establish that there was ordinary negligence by the railroad. The railroad argued that he was a trespasser. The railroad contended that it was not negligent, and that Tompkins was negligent because he admitted that he saw the train's lights and heard its horn. He argued that he had walked on the path many times before the accident and had never had a problem.

The trial judge was Stanley Mandelaum and his charge to the jury was based upon the federal common law standard of liability (ordinary negligence). Since the Pennsylvania legal rule that regarded Tompkins as a trespasser was a judicially created rule, federal common law would be applied, following the legal rule as to which law to apply established in *Swift v. Tyson*. The Pennsylvania legal rule was not considered to be Pennsylvania law because it was not established by legislation or custom.

The jury found that the railroad was negligent, and that Tompkins was not contributorily negligent because he had no reason to anticipate that there would be the black object extending from the railroad car. The jury awarded Tompkins $30,000 (about $600,000 in current value).

6.6 Decision in the *Erie* case in the Court of Appeals

The railroad appealed to the Second Circuit Court of Appeals. The case was heard by a three-judge panel. On the appeal, the railroad challenged the finding that it was negligent, and that the plaintiff Tompkins had not been found to be contributorily negligent. The Court of Appeals, in an opinion written by Judge Thomas Walter Swan, affirmed the decision of the District Court.[90]

In the Court of Appeals, the railroad conceded that federal common law was different from Pennsylvania common law, and it argued for the application of Pennsylvania common law. In affirming the decision of the District Court, the Court of Appeals found that the District Court had properly applied federal common law. The railroad then filed a petition for writ of certiorari (a request that the Supreme Court take the case). The Supreme Court decided to hear the appeal. The Supreme Court has discretion to decide which cases it will hear, and it exercises this discretion by accepting or rejecting the petition for the writ of certiorari.

6.7 Decision in the *Erie* case in the Supreme Court

Swift v. Tyson was established law and had been followed for many years. While there had been dissenting opinions in the 50 years prior to the decision in Erie that had raised doubts about whether federal common law should continue to be applied, such as the dissenting opinion in *Black & White*, it was not generally anticipated that *Swift v. Tyson* would be overruled.[91] The majority opinion for the Supreme Court was written by Justice Louis Brandeis in his last year on the bench. He was undoubtedly influenced by Justice Holmes' dissenting opinion in the *Black & White* case. This was the only time in his career that he announced a Supreme Court about-face (overruling of a precedent).

Justice Holmes in his dissenting opinion in the *Black & White* case had not called for an overruling of *Swift v. Tyson*. His reason for applying state law was on the grounds that the local law where the property was located should be applied if use of the property was the relevant issue. Justice Holmes was recommending that an exception to the general rule established in *Swift v. Tyson* be made for cases involving real property (land).

Justice Brandeis did not hesitate in the *Erie* case in overruling *Swift v. Tyson* and declaring that it was no longer applicable in diversity-of-citizenship cases. In *Erie*, the Supreme Court clearly decided that the law of Pennsylvania should be applied rather than the federal common law.

Tompkins had filed in federal court in order to avoid the unfavorable common law of Pennsylvania that would have been applied to his case if he had filed in state court. Under Pennsylvania law, Tompkins was a trespasser, and he was not entitled to a judgment in his favor when the railroad was not grossly negligent. Under federal common law, the decision in the case could be for Tompkins on the grounds that Erie Railroad Co. had been guilty of ordinary negligence.

In the *Erie* case, there was not a gap in the law. Moreover, this was not an instance of open texture because the law was not vague. The law was settled and had been settled for almost 100 years. Prior to the Erie Doctrine being established, the federal courts in diversity-of-citizenship cases, in accordance with the interpretation of the Judiciary Act in *Swift v. Tyson*, applied state statutes and customs with the force of law but not state-court precedents. If there were no applicable state statute or custom, federal common law rules developed by the federal courts were applied. Many cases had been decided in accordance with federal common law after the decision in *Swift v. Tyson*. There were many diversity-of-citizenship decisions in the federal reports of federal-court cases.

The Erie Doctrine provides, then, that there is no federal common law to be applied in diversity-of-citizenship cases; the law to be applied is the law of the relevant state. In accordance with the Erie Doctrine, the Seventh Circuit Court of Appeals in the *Cincinnati* cases discussed in Chapter Four was quite correct in looking to the law of the State of Indiana in deciding the case. The federal court is supposed to decide diversity-of-citizenship cases as the state court would decide them, so that the decision in the federal court would be substantially the same as it would have been had the case been tried in the state court.

The principle the Supreme Court was concerned about in *Swift v. Tyson* was that the federal court should support and encourage commercial efforts. The principle that the Supreme Court considered significant in the *Erie* case was to ensure the same result in federal court as in state court in order to avoid litigants picking federal court over state court, or vice-versa, based upon a potential different result in their case.

If there were consistent results in both the state and the federal legal systems, certainty and predictability would be enhanced, and litigants would not select a court to sue in based upon differences in the laws in federal court in comparison to state courts (it would reduce forum-shopping). The constitutional argument in the *Erie* case is that only wealthy individuals or companies could afford to move to another state or reincorporate in another state in order to manufacture diversity of citizenship (as Brown & Yellow Taxicab did). For less wealthy litigants, this would constitute, then, a denial of equal protection of the laws.

This change in emphasis is expressed by Justice Brandeis:

"Diversity of citizenship jurisdiction was conferred in order to prevent apprehended discrimination in state courts against those not citizens of the State. *Swift v. Tyson* introduced grave discrimination by non-citizens against citizens. It made rights enjoyed under the unwritten 'general law' vary according to whether enforcement was sought in the state or in the federal court and the privilege of selecting the court in which the right should be determined was conferred upon the non-citizen. Thus, the doctrine rendered it impossible to achieve equal protection of the law. In attempting to promote uniformity of law throughout the United States, the doctrine has prevented uniformity in the administration of the law of the State."[92]

In summary, then, after the decision in *Erie Railroad Co. v. Tompkins*, the federal court does not attempt to discover (or create new) federal common law rules in deciding diversity-of-citizenship cases. Instead, the federal court attempts to decide the case as the state court would decide it by applying state law. State law would include not only statutes and customs but also the common law of the state.

6.8 Concurring Opinion in the *Erie* case

Justice Stanley Reed, filed a concurring opinion in *Erie*, agreeing that *Swift v. Tyson* was no longer acceptable. But he did not think that the rule established in the *Swift* case was unconstitutional. He argued that the decision in *Swift v. Tyson* was just an erroneous interpretation of Section 34 of the Judiciary Act. He did not want to overrule *Swift v. Tyson*.

Instead of holding that *Swift v. Tyson* should be overruled, the Supreme Court could have confined the use of federal common law to commercial cases and restricted its application to personal injury cases (Tompkins's claim is a personal injury claim). Alternatively, it could have held, as Justice Holmes had maintained in his dissenting opinion in the Black & White case that federal common law should not be applied to cases involving real property, including personal injuries that occurred on real property (land is real property, like the land Tompkins was walking on when he was hit by the door of the railroad car). The decision in *Erie* could have been that *Swift* be confined to its original factual situation or area of the law (the law concerning commercial disputes).

6.9 Dissenting opinion in the *Erie* case

Justice Pierce Butler filed a dissenting opinion, in which Justice James McReynolds joined. He suggested that the majority opinion was an example of judicial activism. The parties to the case had not raised the issue of the overruling of *Swift v. Tyson* and it had not been argued in their briefs (the written version of their arguments) or argued at the oral argument in the courtroom. Moreover, the Supreme Court had not given the Department of Justice an opportunity to file a brief in the case (this is generally done when a constitutional issue is being raised).

6.10 Decision in the *Erie* case after the appeal to the Supreme Court

The case was sent back to the Second Circuit Court of Appeals so that it could rule on the law of Pennsylvania. The Court of Appeals reversed the decision of the District Court. It found that Tompkins could not prevail under Pennsylvania law, and it decided the issue in an opinion by Judge Swan in favor of Erie Railroad.[93]

6.11 Overruling prior decisions

The Supreme Court obviously has the authority to overrule prior decisions and create new law in doing so. In a recent study of this practice written by Brandon J. Murrill for the Congressional Research Service, updated on September 24, 2018, the reasons for overruling of precedents are set forth. Among the reasons cited are the following: the quality of the reasoning in the precedent; the unworkability of the rule established in the precedent; inconsistency of the precedent with related decisions; and changes in the society. A factor that would lead the Supreme Court not to overrule the precedent would be the extent of reliance upon the rule established in the precedent.

The study states that anticipating when the Supreme Court will overrule a precedent is difficult. The author includes a survey of the cases overruling precedents that illustrate the factors listed above, with the admonition that the Supreme Court has not provided an exhaustive list of the factors it uses to determine if a precedent should be overruled. Table A-1, entitled "List of Overruled Supreme Court Decisions" lists 141 cases, including the *Erie* case, in which a majority of justices of the Supreme Court explicitly stated that a prior decision was being overruled.[94]

The justices deciding *Erie*, then, are clearly not just calling balls and strikes. They are creating law, by overruling well-established pre-existing law. No umpire would have the authority to change the strike zone. Judges do have the authority to change the legal rules.

6.12 Questions about the *Swift, Erie* and the *Cincinnati* cases

These four decisions—*Swift v. Tyson, Erie Railroad Co. v. Tompkins, and Cincinnati Insurance Co. v. Flanders Electric Motor Service, Inc. (1 and 2)*—all involve, in different ways and in varying circumstances, the question of what the law is and how can it be found or created. More specifically, *Swift* and *Erie* discuss whether the law includes rules derived from judicial decisions as well as from statutes and customs. These cases also involve the question of the source of the pre-existing law to be considered in making a correct decision in a diversity-of-citizenship case in federal court.

The primary issue in *Swift* and *Erie* is whether the federal court should apply federal common law (and it is not clear what the source is for federal common law) or should apply the laws of the state that would be applicable to the particular case had it been brought in the state court. Following the Erie Doctrine, the federal courts in the *Cincinnati* cases attempted to apply Indiana law, but the judges failed to predict accurately what Indiana law would be and they refused to delay making their decision until the Indiana Supreme Court declared what Indiana law was on the subject of interpreting the "sudden and accidental" clause in the insurance policy.

The *Erie* decision may be viewed as weak in its reasoning because the majority opinion finds support for its ruling in only two sources: the dissenting opinion in *Black & White* and a law review article. Neither of these sources would generally be regarded as being sufficiently persuasive to justify overruling *Swift v. Tyson*. When looking for what the state law would be, the general view of the Erie Doctrine is that the federal court should look only to state law (putting aside legislation and self-executing customary rules which are regarded as law according to *Swift v. Tyson*)—the rules established in the precedents of the highest court in the state judicial system. Since the federal court is predicting what the state court might decide, it could be argued that it should consider, in addition to precedents, whether the state court might make a just and/or a wise decision rather than a correct decision.

From the state highest court point of view, for the court to consider whether it should change the pre-existing law, the court must determine whether, and to what extent, and in which regard, the pre-existing law should be changed. Standards for evaluating the pre-existing law, then, are necessarily incorporated into the procedure employed for reaching judicial decisions when the judicial power to modify pre-existing law is being exercised. As mentioned earlier, the judges in the highest court in the state are not only deciding the case before them, but they are also judging the law and the desirability of applying the law in the case they are deciding.

6.13 Applying state law

Going even further, one could ask whether the federal court in applying state law should utilize the same ultimate creative powers that a state court would employ, such as overruling an unsatisfactory precedent. The U.S. Supreme Court has declared that:

> "…state law is to be applied in the federal as well as the state courts and it is the duty of the former in every case to ascertain from all the available data what the state law is and apply it rather than to prescribe a different rule, however superior it may appear from the viewpoint of 'general law' and however much the state rule may have departed from prior decisions of the federal courts."[95]

This means that the federal court must apply a rule of state law even though the highest court in the state has not considered that issue for many years even if an intermediate appellate court or a trial court has.[96]

There is authority for the proposition that the federal court must also follow reported decisions of the state's lower courts.[97] There is even support for the view that the federal court must follow not only the legal rules established in the decisions of state courts but also "considered dicta."[98] Dicta is language in the opinion that is not relevant to the precedential value of the decision. In the decision about following dicta, the court stated that "the responsibility of the federal courts, in matters of local law, is not to formulate the legal mind of the state, but merely to ascertain and apply it."[99] But the theories expressed in this paragraph are not the prevailing opinion about the Erie Doctrine.

In summary, my view is that the duty of the federal court according to the Erie Doctrine is to reach a correct decision. It is solely that of discovering and applying the applicable state law as found in the decisions of the highest court in the state, and the federal court is not authorized to remold or reformulate this state law in deciding the case in federal court.

6.14 Economics and the wise decision

Some legal philosophers contend that policies or goals, such as the desirability of promoting commerce could, or should, be considered in making judicial decisions. They maintain that economic factors should be an important consideration in the reaching of judicial decisions.[100]

Richard A. Posner, a legal philosopher who has written many books and who served as a judge on the Court of Appeals for many years but is now retired, supports a pragmatic decision-making theory.[101] His theory is different from my version of the wise decision because Posner suggests that all decisions should be pragmatic.[102] I view reaching a wise decision, even if it is pragmatic, as reflecting only one of the three elements involved in reaching a judicial decision, to wit, only looking at the wise decision. Posner does, however, accept that correct decisions are justified, and he could be interpreted as considering the just decision and the wise decision to both be pragmatic decisions.[103]

6.15 Describing the wise decision

The idea that judges act like umpires calling balls and strikes when they decide cases is a return to the traditional theory that judges do not make the law but discover it. The proponents of the traditional theory support the notion that all that judges do is discover the law and apply it in a mechanical way to the factual situation to arrive at a decision. They accept that making judicial decisions is similar to an umpire calling balls and strikes. The traditional theory lost favor around the middle of the twentieth century and few knowledgeable persons continue to support the traditional theory

The change in the general understanding of what judges actually do is primarily the result of the theories expressed by some of the American Legal Realists, such as Jerome Frank. These realists rejected the traditional theory because they believe that judges do not decide cases by applying the legal rules and they offer a variety of theories about what judges do. Having accomplished this important task, their influence waned. Legal philosophy was then dominated by the legal positivists.

Legal positivists, in general, accept the idea that there can be a correct decision, but they would not agree, except in rare instances, that other factors besides the pre-existing law enter into the judicial process. They accept the incorrect decision by mistake but do not generally discuss the just decision or the wise decision. I mention the history of legal philosophy here because there does not appear to be today universal acceptance of any of these schools of jurisprudence and probably none of the historical theories is consistent with the theory that I am suggesting. I will compare my theory, creative positivism with other legal theories in *The Judge and the Philosopher*.

According to the traditional theory, the judge in making his decision never considers policy issues, such as the prospective consequences of the legal rule that is being applied to the factual situation to decide the case and the judge also does not consider whether the decision will be a just decision. I supplement the correct decision in which the legal rules of the pre-existing law are applied with the alternate source decision (which could be the just decision or the wise decision). It is my belief that judges do in fact consider alternate sources in reaching judicial decisions, though the alternate sources may lead to the same decision as the correct decision.

The consideration of policy would include weighing the principles that underpin the legal rules. These principles could be expressions of publicly held values (all persons should be treated equally, for example) or summary statements of the reason for a legal rule or a group of legal rules (recognition of the right of privacy, for example). The wise decision could also include consideration of the effect of the decision upon not only the individuals in the case but also on the wider society and the desirability of the proposed rule established by the decision as a precedent.

The wise decision may include, in addition to principles and the consideration of the consequences of the decision, goals and values. The judge making an alternate source decision that is not a correct decision is making law, exercising a special form of quasi-legislative judgment and attempting to frame a legal rule that will achieve beneficial results. There is a sense in which every decision involves judgment, and one could agree that applying a law involves making a judgment call. But there is a vast difference between the judgment involved in applying a law and the evaluation of the justice or wisdom of a particular judicial decision by a judge.

To make the wise decision requires consideration of the beneficial social effects of the decision being made and the legal rule that the decision in the instant case will create if the decision is also not a correct decision. In determining the beneficial social effects, the value of the rule established by the decision that will act as a controlling force of human behavior within the society and as a guide to future judges should be studied, weighed and evaluated. To decide which social effects would be beneficial requires review of which social policies will be prudent and advantageous policies for the society in question.

There is great disagreement about which policies will be prudent and advantageous. Each person will consider a decision unwise if it neglects or disregards values which he believes are important and essential to the well-being of the society. For the purposes of presenting this theory of justification for judicial decisions, we do not need either to exercise a choice about which ends would be desirable or choose a method for determining their desirability, such as, for example, utilitarianism or pragmatism. All we need to agree upon is that the social effects of the decision should be a consideration in reaching the decision. In short, we just must accept that the judge is not just calling balls and strikes—he is making law.

The judge has reached a correct decision when the law, which is the body of legal rules in existence before the judge decides the case, is applied to decide the case. The judge, however, may also reach a decision that is inconsistent with the pre-existing law, that one could characterize as an incorrect decision. The federal court that applies the pre-existing law of a particular state to decide a diversity-of-citizenship case will reach a correct decision when it accurately applies the law of the relevant state to decide the case. The state court that hears a similar case may elect to make a decision that is not consistent with the pre-existing law because it wants to create an exception to the rule, or it wants to modify the rule in some other significant way. The state court may conclude that the preferable course of action is to reach a more desirable decision than the correct decision even though that decision would not be a correct decision.

I have presented the *Cincinnati 1* case in order to provide a concrete illustration of an incorrect decision. Also, the case allows me to discuss a second type of decision that is also inconsistent with the pre-existing law, so that I may distinguish the two types of incorrect decisions.

Cincinnati 1 represents one type of decision that is not correct. This is a situation in which the Court of Appeals concluded (by research or guestimate) that the Indiana Supreme Court would resolve the issue one way, but the Indiana Supreme Court decided the issue the contrary way. This decision by the federal court I call an incorrect decision by mistake.

Erie Railroad Co. v. Tompkins is my example of the second type of decision that is not consistent with pre-existing law. In *Erie*, the United States Supreme Court decided that the decision in *Swift v. Tyson* should be overruled. This was not a correct decision in the sense that it was not consistent with established law. The inconsistency, however, is not a result of the Supreme Court making a mistake as to what was the established legal rule.

Instead, this was a deliberate action taken to change the law, which could be considered in some respects to be comparable to a legislature repealing one statute and adopting another one. In one quick stroke, the Supreme Court changed the rules completely and wiped out, for all practical purposes, close to 100 years of decided cases, by dismissing the entire body of general federal common law previously used to decide diversity-of-citizenship cases. *Erie* is clearly not an instance of a court resolving an issue of unsettled law or filling a gap in the law or even deciding a case on the edges of a legal rule (in the penumbra).

You may wonder whether the cases decided pursuant to the body of legal rules that were the established law during the one-hundred-year reign of *Swift v. Tyson* can now be reversed if the applicable state law at the time the case was decided would require a different result. The response to this inquiry is that the finality-of-decision doctrine employed by the Court of Appeals in *Cincinnati 2* would preclude such a result. All these decisions, whether decided in accordance with or contrary to state law when they were decided, are still binding decisions in regard to the parties in those cases, even though the decisions themselves are no longer precedents. These decisions are, therefore, binding but not authoritative.

A different question might be whether the cases we are reviewing support the position of Jerome N. Frank that there are no rules of law because the law consists of only the actual decisions:

> "All decisions are law. The fact that courts render these decisions makes them law. There is no mysterious entity apart from these decisions. If the judges in any case come to a 'wrong' result and give forth a decision which is discordant with their own or anyone else's rules, their decision is none the less law."[104]

I disagree with this contention because I want to acknowledge that courts can reach correct decisions, but I agree that, once the decision is made, the decision applies the law or creates new law.

A third question could be whether the decisions decided pursuant to *Swift v. Tyson* should now be regarded as incorrect decisions, and, because they are incorrect decisions, we should declare that they are invalid decisions. If you follow Frank's reasoning, the judges cannot make incorrect decisions since their decisions are the law. If you disagree with Frank and accept that judges may decide cases consistent with or inconsistent with. pre-existing law, it does not follow those incorrect decisions will be invalid decisions. Instead, I maintain that even incorrect decisions (and I do regard, as I have said, both *Cincinnati 1* and *Erie* to be decisions that are not correct, though they are different types of incorrect decisions) are authorized and binding. *Cincinnati 1* is not authoritative because it has no impact upon Indiana law, while *Erie* is authoritative as the *Cincinnati* cases demonstrate because they followed the Erie Doctrine.

A fourth question might be whether the decisions that were decided in accordance with a mistakenly developed federal common law used to decide diversity-of-citizenship cases are decisions that should be regarded as null and void *ab initio*.[105] In other words, they might be invalid when they were made (not just potentially invalid because the

Erie case overruled *Swift v. Tyson*). There is no basis, however, for such a conclusion. Since the decisions in question were decided in accordance with the law as it existed when they were decided, they would be valid decisions, and they will remain valid decisions until such time as a later court determines to the contrary.

The bottom line is that a decision has to be made in a case that is filed in court even if the decision is that the court will not hear the case and will dismiss it without really acting upon the merits of the case.[106] Even this decision will be authorized, authoritative, and binding (until such time and only if it is reversed by a second agency which has authority to reverse it).

Ultimately, every decision is eligible to be viewed as being a correct decision or an incorrect decision. It cannot be both correct and incorrect. This is an either-or proposition. It is illogical to assert that a decision for either the plaintiff or the defendant could both be a correct decision. This is fundamental for analysis of judicial decisions.

The most importance difference between the umpire and the judge is that the judge can change the rules of the game, and the umpire has no such authority. In fact, and to go even further, published judicial decisions may change the legal rules. The similarity between judges and umpires is that both make decisions that you could refer to as judgment calls in applying the applicable rules. But, once again, judges have authority to change the rules and umpires have no authority to do so.

6.16 One final statement about the *Erie* case

In an article written in 1938 by a professor at Yale Law School about *Swift v. Tyson* and *Erie Railroad Co. v. Tompkins*, there is an eloquent description of the role of judges. Professor Harry Shulman asks the question whether federal judges in applying state law, such as required by the *Erie* case after the Supreme Court's decision, will not be able to exercise the same degree of judicial craftsmanship as Pennsylvania judges would demonstrate if they were deciding the case:

"If the answer to the foregoing question is 'yes,' the federal judges are, for the first time in one hundred and fifty years, limited in a way in which the Pennsylvania judges are not themselves limited. The common law of Pennsylvania, like its statutory and constitutional law, is an evolutionary and variable product. In the main, it is the creative work of the judges, dealing with the living stream of dispute and conflict, searching in each new litigated case for a reasonable and working guide to a solution. The guide is a rule of law, a generalization drawn from life history, one that is so well drawn from that history that it will successfully meet the pragmatic test of explanatory rationalization. The judge's work in constructing this generalization instantly becomes a part of the history that will be used by the judges in succeeding cases; it is one new step in the evolution of the law. Every new case has some new factors that require original consideration by the court. In some sense, every new case is a case 'of first impression.'

"In dealing with each new controversy, the Pennsylvania judge must search for the applicable law, not merely in earlier Pennsylvania cases, nor merely in the various customs of Philadelphia and Pittsburgh or Bryn Mawr. He looks for enlightening direction to the decisions and doctrines and custom of England, old and new, of other states and countries, of other courts, federal or state or foreign. He is not hindered by any antecedent doctrine, itself man-made by some judge or jurist like himself. Of course, he weighs all such doctrines with constructive and respectful care and passes his independent judgment as to which form of worded rule will best serve for the solution of his immediate problem. He is far from certain of finding this worded rule in the opinions of Pennsylvania courts alone."[107]

I have included this statement because this professor from Yale Law School created a picture of judicial craftsmanship that is far different from that described by Justice Kavanaugh, who graduated from Yale Law School and compared judges to umpires 80 years after this was written. Shulman's observation is that the Erie Doctrine would require the federal courts in diversity-of-citizenship cases to make only correct decisions and that this would result in inconsistency between the law of the state and the law that the federal courts would apply. It was the effort to avoid this inconsistency that was the goal of the Supreme Court in establishing the Erie Doctrine.

In *Cincinnati 1*, the federal court was applying the law of the state of Indiana to decide the case. The federal court was not creating a new legal rule to apply in future cases and not creating a binding precedent for the Indiana courts. The federal court was applying Indiana law in disregard of whether the Indiana Supreme Court would make a wise decision. This is a critical shortcoming of the Erie Doctrine. The Indiana Supreme Court was creating a binding precedent and, in doing so, it would necessarily consider the consequences of its decision.

As the law of Indiana developed, the Indiana Supreme Court wanted to provide insurance coverage and require that the insurance company pay for the environmental remediation. The goal was to protect the environment and provide the insurance coverage to do so. These are real consequences of their decision, but they were not considered to be relevant in the federal court, which only had to make a correct decision regardless of the consequences of the decision. There are, in effect, no consequences to be considered by the federal court (other than the impact on the parties before the court) since the decision would not be a precedent.

I now want to consider two more cases. The first case in Chapter Seven was decided by the courts in Pennsylvania at the trial level, the intermediate appellate level and by the Pennsylvania Supreme Court, which made a correct, unjust, wise decision. The second case in Chapter Eight went through all three levels of the federal judicial system and the U.S. Supreme Court made an incorrect, unjust, wise decision.

7.
THE CORRECT, UNJUST, WISE DECISION

CONWAY V. CUTLER GROUP—THE IMPLIED WARRANTY OF HABITABILITY CASE

7.1 The facts in *Conway v. Cutler Group*

In September 2003, the Field family (David and Holly Field) purchased a new house constructed by the Cutler Group. After living there for three years, the Field family sold the house to the Conway family in June 2006. In April 2008, the Conways (Michael and Deborah Conway) discovered there was water infiltration around some of the windows in the house and they hired an engineering and architectural firm that advised them that there were construction defects that were causing the damage. In June 2011, the Conways sued the Cutler Group. The damage was quite extensive and the cost to repair the house would be very expensive.[108]

The lawsuit was based upon whether Conway could claim that the builder had breached the implied warranty of habitability.[109] The basic policy of the common law is the traditional doctrine of *caveat emptor*, which provides that, if there is no fraud or misrepresentation, then the general policy is *caveat emptor* (buyer beware). This means that the seller is not responsible for the quality of the item being sold. In

Pennsylvania, however, there was a well-established exception to this general rule of the common law.

In the case of *Elderkin v. Gaster*, the Pennsylvania Supreme Court had established the doctrine of the implied warranty of habitability. Both *caveat emptor* and the implied warranty of habitability are judicially created legal norms. The Supreme Court reasoned in the *Elderkin* case that, when the doctrine of *caveat emptor* was established, buyers and sellers were on relatively equal footing, and they had equivalent knowledge and bargaining power. The purchase price agreed upon theoretically was based upon their mutual knowledge and reflected any defects in the item being sold.

When considering the purchase of a recently constructed house, however, the parties are not equal. The builder is supposedly highly skilled, and the purchaser relies upon the skill of the builder in making the purchase. The implied warranty of habitability provides that, when a new home is constructed, the builder impliedly warrants (promises) that the home has been constructed in a reasonably workmanlike manner and that it is habitable (one may live in it). If it is not habitable, the builder is legally liable for the cost of repair. Therefore, the builder assumes the risk of any defects that are a result of the house not being properly constructed. The warranty is, in effect, the court-imposed contractual promise from the builder to the purchaser that the house will be free of defects. It is an "implied warranty," which means that the court is placing the warranty in the contract between the parties as though they had agreed upon it.

7.2 The trial court decision in *Conway v. Cutler Group*

Notwithstanding the implied warranty of habitability established in the *Elderkin* case, the Court of Common Pleas in Bucks County, Pennsylvania, in an opinion by Judge Clyde Waite, in the *Conway* case, decided the case in favor of the builder. The trial court distinguished *Elderkin* because in that case the builder had sold the house to the plaintiff (the party filing the lawsuit) who had been the first purchaser of the house. In the *Conway* case, there had been no contractual relationship between the builder and the Conways, so that, lacking such a contract, there was no contract in which the warranty could be implied. In other words, the plaintiffs, the Conways, had no cause of action that would support the lawsuit. The trial court reasoned that the question of who should bear the burden of damages for the construction defects was a question, ultimately, of public policy.[110]

Judge Waite considered the public policy issue, and this is his approach to it:

> "The public policy to place the burden of risk on the builder by extending the impliedly contracted for warranty of habitability has not yet been established. The builder is not a guarantor or warrantor for all buyers within the line of title based on the original contract of warranty. As a matter of public policy, this issue is of particular importance in light of the common practice of insurers to exclude latent defects in coverage questions for property insurance. The issue then is one of policy of who will bear the burden of damages caused by latent defects not reasonably discoverable by prudent buyers of relatively new residential dwellings."[111]

The court did not discuss whether the decision would be just or unjust. The judge also did not decide what the public policy should be. He declined to modify or extend the implied warranty of habitability that had been created by the Supreme Court in the *Elderkin* case.

7.3 The Pennsylvania Superior Court decision in *Conway v. Cutler Group*

The Conways appealed to the Pennsylvania Superior Court, which is an intermediate appellate court. In a unanimous result, the Superior Court, in an opinion by Judge Sallie Updyke Mundy, for a three-judge panel, reversed the trial court and found in favor of the Conways. The Superior Court agreed with the trial court that the implied warranty of habitability is based upon public policy considerations. The doctrine of the implied warranty of habitability, according to the Superior Court, was created by the courts in order to equalize the disproportionate advantage of the builder in comparison to the house purchaser. It is not based upon and does not require that there be a contract between the builder and the plaintiffs who were not the first purchaser of the house.[112]

The Superior Court cited two precedents decided after the decision in *Elderkin*. There was a case before the Superior Court 18 years after the *Elderkin* case in which the first purchaser was a property management company, which never occupied the house. The Superior Court held that the implied warranty of habitability would protect the first user-purchaser, who had purchased the house from the property management company. The property management company was the first purchaser, but it had never occupied the house.[113]

The second case was a Court of Common Pleas (which is the trial court in Pennsylvania) decision that extended the implied warranty of habitability to a second purchaser when the first purchaser had no knowledge of the latent defect. The trial court found that the transaction between the first purchaser and the second purchaser reflected an assumption based upon the price paid for the house that the house had no latent construction defects.[114] Since this was a decision by a court that was lower than the Superior Court in the hierarchy of Pennsylvania courts, the decision would not be regarded as a binding precedent in the Superior Court. The Superior Court, however, cited this case with apparent approval.

The Superior Court viewed the *Conway* case as involving which party should be responsible for the cost of repair as between a builder and a house purchaser. Judge Mundy posed the question of which party should bear the burden of that cost:

"As between the builder-vendor [the builder-seller] and the vendee [the purchaser], the position of the former, even though he exercises reasonable care, dictates that he bears the risk that a home which he has built will be functional and habitable in accordance with contemporary community standards. We thus hold that the builder-vendor impliedly warrants that the home he has built and is selling is constructed in a reasonably workmanlike manner and that it is fit for the purpose intended habitation."[115]

Framing the decision in terms that echo those of the just decision, the Superior Court viewed a decision in favor of the Conways as the best decision:

"It seems only fair to put the burden of repairing defects in construction on the person who is (1) responsible for the defects, (2) is in a position to repair them and (3) is in a position to spread the costs of repair. This is especially true since a significant amount of the defects can be so buried in the construction that it could be impossible to find them before buying, no matter how careful or thorough the inspection."

The Superior Court did not view the implied warranty of habitability as being based on either contract law or contractual promises from the builder. Hence, the Superior Court reversed the decision of the trial court and decided in favor of the Conways. The Superior Court agreed with the trial court that the case involved a question of public policy and that to decide for the builder "would present problematic consequences." It appears that the Superior Court was making an incorrect, just and, in the opinion of Judge Mundy, wise decision.

7.4 The decision of the Pennsylvania Supreme Court in *Conway v. Cutler Group*

The builder in the *Conway* case then filed an appeal to the Pennsylvania Supreme Court from the decision of the Superior Court. The description of the issue before the Supreme Court on the appeal is the following:

> "Did the Superior Court wrongly decide an important question of first impression in Pennsylvania when it held that any subsequent purchaser of a used residence may recover damages for breach of the builder implied warranty of habitability to new home purchasers?"[116]

The phrase "case of first impression" is used when the exact issue presented has never been considered by the court.

The Supreme Court reversed the decision of the Superior Court and reinstated the decision of the trial court in favor of the builder. The Supreme Court read *Elderkin* as a breach of contract case. Since there was no contract between the builder and the Conways, this was the primary distinguishing factor between the *Elderkin* and the *Conway* cases—they were not "like" factual situations but were, according to the Supreme Court, different regarding this significant factual distinction. There was a contract in *Elderkin* between the builder and the purchaser of the house, and such a contract was lacking in *Conway*, which was fatal to the Conway's claim.[117]

In refusing to extend the implied warranty of habitability to a situation where the house had been occupied for several years and the parties in the lawsuit had not contracted with each other, the Supreme Court held that the builder had no liability for the latent defects in the house that the Conways had purchased. They had not purchased the house from the builder, so the builder could not be found to be liable for a breach of the implied warranty of habitability.

The two cases cited by the Superior Court, which were not binding precedents in the Supreme Court because they were decided by inferior courts in the hierarchy of the judicial system, were distinguished by the Supreme Court. In the first case, the plaintiff purchased a house that had not yet been built and, while he was not a first purchaser of the house, the first purchaser had never used or occupied the house. Therefore, the second purchaser, the plaintiff, was viewed as the *de facto* equivalent of a first purchaser. This was a very narrow extension of the legal rule applied in the *Elderkin* case by including a second purchaser who was the first user of the house within the scope of the judicially created implied warranty of habitability.

Since the question of whether the builder could be found to be liable for breach of the implied warranty of habitability when the plaintiff is not a first purchaser or first user had never been considered in Pennsylvania by either the Superior Court or the Supreme Court before the *Conway* case, the Supreme Court did look at the decisions in other states (which are not controlling decisions in Pennsylvania) for guidance. The Supreme Court cited decisions made by appellate courts in Iowa, Rhode Island, Vermont and Connecticut.

The holding of the Supreme Court in favor of the builder in the *Conway* case is explained in this way:

> "After careful review of the arguments of the parties, the comments of amici [this is a reference to the individuals and organizations who are not parties in the case but who had filed *amicus curie* briefs, friend of the court briefs, expressing their opinion about how the case should be decided], and the reasoned decisions of our sister states on this issue, we conclude that the question of whether and/or under what circumstances to extend an implied warranty of habitability to subsequent purchasers of a newly constructed residence is a matter of public policy properly left to the General Assembly [the Pennsylvania legislature]."[118]

The Supreme Court viewed the arguments that were presented to the Supreme Court as based upon policy considerations that necessitated extensive fact-finding and weighing of potential consequences. This type of inquiry required the kind of law-creation reserved to the legislature and the issue was not suitable for judicial action. The Supreme Court was emphasizing that the ability of the judiciary to decide policy issues is limited.[119]

While no one would argue that the authority of the judiciary to decide issues of public policy has no limits, there is no red line between the limit on the court of deciding policy issues and the authority to make the wise decision (and, also, the just decision). I have cited the *Erie* case and the *Conway* case as examples of the wise decision having been made by courts in which the consideration of public policy was involved, though, in *Erie* the court made the policy decision and in *Conway* it declined to do so. In fact, it was the policy judgment of the courts that was the basis for both decisions, including the judicial policy of whether the court should decide the public policy issue. The same may be said of *Mosser v. Darrow*, which is the next case that we will consider.

Bear in mind that the doctrine of the implied warranty of habitability, and the policy underlying that doctrine, was established by the judiciary. In *Elderkin*, the Supreme Court was inspired by its concept of the relevant public policy in order to create the legal norm that is the implied warranty of habitability. Having established that legal norm, the Supreme Court is now refusing in the *Conway* case to extend its judicially created legal norm. We could argue whether or not extending the legal norm would be a wise decision. The difficulty here is that there is no clear guidepost to provide the basis for when the wise decision should be or should not be made, and you may consider the refusal to consider the wise decision to be itself a wise decision. I will return to this issue below.

In short, the law is not clearly established by the Supreme Court of Pennsylvania regarding which policy issues should be left to the legislature. As far as the issue in the *Conway* case is concerned, this is not an issue that would give rise to the jurisdiction of the United States Supreme Court, so that the Supreme Court of Pennsylvania is the highest court in the land in the State of Pennsylvania.

7.5 The court is not the legislature

There is little reason to spend much time on establishing that courts are not legislatures. Courts do not have the resources to study policy issues; they are limited by the trickle of cases in a specific confined area of the law being presented in an unorganized and haphazard manner; and their fundamental role is to resolve disputes though they also have a role in regulating the behavior of those subjected to the law or those utilizing the law to accomplish social results. Bear in mind that the individual judge and even panels of judges are not systemically coordinating the flow of cases.

For lower-court judges, following the legal rules established in the precedents of the superior courts is based upon one or some of the following reasons: the easiest way to do their jobs (the most efficient course of action); the way to avoid having their decisions reversed; implementing the obligation to apply the law in deciding cases; applying legal rules pronounced by higher courts is a policy-oriented strategy; and acting in a way that is compatible with the judge's view of the role of judges in the legal system.

Appellate judges have more discretion than trial-court judges. Therefore, appellate judges have more opportunity to create legal rules. But no judge has the authority to create legal rules in the same manner as a legislature. Courts are more limited in their authority to create law and even more limited in their opportunity to do so.

7.6 The role of policy

I am using the term "policy" to include policies, principles, standards, and values. Policy is part of the element of the wise decision. The wise decision could also be the result of applying the law (the wise decision could also be the correct decision).

Every law, each legal norm, will have a purpose, sometimes explicit and other times implicit. For example, the legal norm could be "in order to improve worker safety, every worker in the factory must wear a hard hat." Here, the purpose is clear. Some laws could have multiple purposes. There should be no conflict between the purpose(s) and the legal norm, unless there is a gross example of sloppy drafting of the language of the legal norm. The purpose of the legal norm is based upon the anticipated consequences of the legal norm.

The purpose of a legal norm, however, has only a small degree of influence on the interpretation of the legal norm, even though it could be considered to be part of applying the legal norm in order to make the correct decision. The purpose of the rule is often unclear, it may conflict with other values of the legal system, the rule can be over-inclusive or underinclusive in relation to the rule's supposed purpose, the rule may result in consequences that are contrary to the rule's purpose, or the rule may result in unintended consequences or unthought of consequences.

The legal system reflects many policies. These policies may conflict with each other. The laws themselves, however, never conflict in the sense that disputes must be resolved, correct decisions are presumptively justified, and correct decisions are made by applying the pre-existing law. If there is a potential conflict in the legal norms, it is resolved by applying the legal norm that is most applicable. There is always a potential legal norm to apply to resolve every dispute because the law is coherent, comprehensive, complete, gapless and consistent so that, in making the judicial decision, the decision necessarily eliminates any potential conflict among the rules. There is never a tie; every case will result in a decision.

Policies will be a factor in the legal system in many ways, though policies may conflict with each other. The element of the wise decision presupposes that there is a best decision. The best decision may be an alternate source decision (the just decision and/or the wise decision). In order to make the wise decision, policies must be evaluated. For the wise decision to be compared to the correct decision, the legal norm that would result in the correct decision has to be evaluated. The correct decision is the decision that would be made by applying pre-existing law with no requirement of evaluation of the legal norm to be applied to do so.

There are policies embedded in the law (in the legal norms). There are also policies inherent in the legal system. These are all public policies. These policies, from their multiple sources, could conflict. The wise decision must resolve that conflict, by selecting from among the policies. The decision to avoid making the policy decision (as in the *Conway* case) is itself the implementation of a policy, to wit, the policy to leave policy decisions to the legislature.

The irony in the *Conway* case is that the question of whether the court should make a policy decision or whether it should avoid making a policy decision is itself a policy decision. In other words, the decision not to make a decision is a decision made pursuant to a court-made policy as to which cases it should decide on their merits and which cases are not worthy of being decided on their merits (the decision to decide the case is avoided by applying a rule to allow for avoiding a decision on the merits of the case). The correct decision in the *Conway* case allows the court to avoid making a policy decision as to whether or whether not the home builder should be liable for the defects in the house it built.

In the *Elderkin* case, the decision was made to adopt a policy to protect home purchasers who had less bargaining power and knowledge than home builders, by creating the implied warranty of habitability. Thus, the Supreme Court in the *Elderkin* case created a legal norm, which the Supreme Court declined to modify but which it left intact in the *Conway* case.

7.7 Hypothetical example of conflicting policies

Let me now present a hypothetical example of how policies might conflict. Mary uses the social security checks she and her husband Hank receive to purchase pain-killing medicine for Hank. Hank is suffering from cancer and is projected to have 6 to 12 months to live. They have no other source of income. As a result of purchasing the expensive medicine, Mary is unable to make the mortgage payments to Customers Bank. The bank forecloses on the mortgage and Mary asks Judge Gray to stay the foreclosure (to not let it proceed for a period of time) until after Hank's death and she will then try to bring the mortgage current. The bank opposes her request.

Judge Gray is very compassionate, and he understands Mary's dilemma and why she chose to purchase the medicine rather than pay the mortgage. He thinks that deciding in Mary's favor would be the just decision. A decision for Mary, however, could result in the bank in the future refusing to grant mortgages to people who have or have had cancer. Banks are reluctant to grant mortgages to borrowers who will be unable to make the mortgage payments. Customers Bank is a small bank in a small community.

Depositors, when they learn that their bank is unable to foreclose on mortgages, may withdraw their funds in their savings accounts. They could be concerned that the bank might fail when the bank cannot collect mortgage payments and cannot proceed with mortgage foreclosures.

Other creditors may be faced with a similar inability to collect on their loans or on their invoices if the court makes a decision in their case similar to the potential decision for Mary in Mary's case. Judge Gray is concerned that a decision for Mary is a slippery slope and that he might, if he decides for Mary, create an avalanche of unintended consequences. In other words, Judge Gray recognizes that even the just decision has consequences beyond what is just for the parties in the case.

While Judge Gray is sympathetic to Mary's plight, and he himself would make the same decision she is making if he were in her place, he must consider the consequences of his decision. He wants to make the just decision and the wise decision, but a decision for Mary could foster undesirable results and be an unwise decision.

This is obviously a conflict of policies, and even of values, and there is no easy answer. The Supreme Court of Pennsylvania was confronted with a similar dilemma in *Elderkin* and then in *Conway*. Every line of cases creating a new legal norm starts somewhere with a court making a decision that might be a wise decision in creating the new legal rule, such as the new legal rule called the implied warranty of habitability that was created in the *Elderkin* case. The decision will be a precedent and the legal rule upon which the decision is based will have consequences, some intended and some unintended. Later decisions will expand the rule, like when the implied warranty of habitability was extended to the second purchaser when the first purchaser did not occupy the house. Other decisions, such as in the *Conway* case, will not expand the rule and will confine it to a more limited class of potential litigants.

As Karl Llewellyn, a professor of law and one of the most influential members of the American Legal Realists, points out, judges are concerned about a good society and a better law in their decision-making, which guides them in the creation of new law.[120] Justice Holmes believes that the justification of any rule of law is that it helps to bring about a desired social end.[121] Consideration of the wise decision forces judges and critics of judicial decisions to reflect upon policies and consequences.

Therefore, there is potential tension between the law (the correct decision) and the alternate source decision (the wise decision or the just decision). In order to make the alternate source decision, public policy must be considered, and courts do consider public policy when they make such just and wise decisions. This will become more evident in *Mosser v. Darrow*, the next case that we will consider.

8.
THE INCORRECT, UNJUST, WISE DECISION

MOSSER V. DARROW—LIABILITY OF THE TRUSTEE EVEN THOUGH HE RECEIVED NO PERSONAL BENEFIT

8.1 Facts of the *Mosser v. Darrow* case

Federal Facilities Realty Trust and National Realty Trust filed for bankruptcy reorganization in 1934. The two trusts constructed and owned buildings that were leased to the U.S. Postal Service. The buildings were built with bond financing. The U.S. Postal Service decided to start building its own buildings, which adversely impacted the business of the two trusts.

Paul E. Darrow was appointed by the bankruptcy court to be the trustee of the two trusts. Jacob Kulp and Myrtle Johnson were two key employees of the two trusts. In fact, they had organized the two trusts. Kulp was originally hired in 1929 and he was a contractor who had constructed the buildings owned by the trusts. Johnson managed the office of the two trusts. She was responsible for buying the bonds of the trusts when they came on the market. She established the price that the trusts would pay for these bonds. Kulp and Johnson also owned some of the bonds on their own account.

Darrow was advised by a former trustee of the two trusts that he should hire Kulp and Johnson to help him manage the affairs of the two trusts. Darrow considered Kulp and Johnson to be indispensable for the effective management of the trusts. Pursuant to the order of the District Court, Darrow hired them, and they became part-time employees and worked out of the office of the two trusts. From the beginning, Kulp continued to manage the physical properties and Johnson to supervise the office activities.

Johnson and Kulp were partners in their own business activities for their mutual account. These two individuals would work for the trusts only if the trustee would agree that they could speculate for their own account in the bonds of the two trusts. The trustee acquiesced to this condition of their employment.

The two employees made a considerable profit as a result of their speculation in the bonds of the two trusts. They knew how the business worked and they were familiar with many of the bondholders. On some occasions, Johnson and Kulp acquired bonds for themselves, and, on the same day, or within a few days, they transferred the bonds to the trusts at a profit. In some cases, these bonds were bought from bondholders who came to the office of the trusts to offer to sell their bonds. Johnson and Kulp shared that office with the two trusts and met the bondholders there and bought some of these bonds for their own account.

Darrow bought the bonds of the trusts for retirement when he could purchase them at a discount. Darrow relied on Johnson's advice in allocating funds for these purchases and the prices to be offered for the bonds. The bonds were bought at market price, and, except for one purchase, they were worth more when Darrow resigned as the trustee than he had paid for them. The two trusts made a large profit (indebtedness of $2.5 million was reduced by these purchases), but the two trusts would have realized an even larger profit if the two employees had not purchased the bonds for their own account.

Darrow, the trustee, received no personal gain or compensation related to the purchases by the two trusts or the speculation in the bonds by the two employees.

In 1943, Darrow filed his final reports as trustee. Stacy C. Mosser was appointed as a replacement trustee, and she filed objections to the final reports of the two trusts. Many objections were minor, but Mosser objected to the profits made by Kulp and Johnson in their dealings with purchasing and selling the bonds on their own account.

8.2 The District Court decision in *Mosser v. Darrow*

The District Court found that Darrow was guilty of wrongdoing or negligence as a trustee and entered a surcharge order in the amount of $43,442 against Darrow for the amount of profit the trusts would have made had Kulp and Johnson not been allowed to speculate in the bonds of the two trusts.[122] A surcharge order is a court order that imposes an obligation upon a party, which in this case was the obligation to reimburse the two trusts for the profit that the two trusts would have made except for the activities of the two employees.

8.3 The Court of Appeals decision in *Mosser v. Darrow*

Darrow appealed to the 7th Circuit Court of Appeals. Darrow contended that there were no precedents in which a trustee had been surcharged when the trustee himself had not profited and had not participated in any way to defraud the trust. Mosser, the successor trustee, cited cases from England going back to 1794. The Court of Appeals reviewed the old English cases and concluded that there was no liability when there was no fraud. The English courts were concerned that no one would serve as a trustee if they could be held liable for the acts of their employees even though they received no benefit from those acts. The Court of Appeals held that the general rule was that a trustee is not liable for the misdeeds of his agents so long as he exercised reasonable care.

The three-judge panel in the 7th Circuit Court of Appeals unanimously held that the law in the United States was similar to that in England. The Court of Appeals reversed the decision of the District Court and held that Darrow could not be surcharged.[123] The reasoning of the Court of Appeals was that trustees cannot operate businesses without expert help. Darrow was not negligent in hiring the general manager and bookkeeper/office manager. He acted in good faith and used ordinary care and prudence in managing the trusts.

According to the Court of Appeals, a trustee is not liable for the fraudulent acts of his employees. A trustee is liable for surcharge only when he himself is guilty of fraud or negligence. The Court of Appeals held that Mosser, the successor trustee, could not cite a single relevant precedent supporting the surcharge. Mosser filed an appeal to the Supreme Court.

8.4 The majority opinion in the U.S. Supreme Court in *Mosser v. Darrow*

The Supreme Court was faced, on the one hand, with the problem of constructing a rule that would lend itself to practical application in the future and the realization that the application of this rule in the case before the Supreme Court, on the other hand, should be a fair rule to apply to the facts in the instant case. In other words, application of the rule to be crafted by the Supreme Court imposing the surcharge might lead the Supreme Court, and the Supreme Court expressly admitted this, though not in this terminology, to an unjust, wise decision. The Supreme Court reversed the Court of Appeals and held that Darrow was liable for the loss suffered by the two trusts as a result of the fraudulent acts of the two employees, even though Darrow himself did not profit from their fraud.[124]

Justice Robert H. Jackson delivered the majority opinion for the Supreme Court. He framed the issue as whether the Supreme Court could find personal liability of a reorganization trustee who, although making no personal profit, permitted key employees to profit from trading in the bonds of the two trusts. The Supreme Court held that the District Court "was correct and the decision of the Court of Appeals cannot stand."[125]

8.5 The dissenting opinion in *Mosser v. Darrow*

In those cases where the application of the legal rule of the pre-existing law does not lead to a satisfactory result, the creation of the rule that would lead to a wise decision may not lead to a just result in the case before the court. One possible solution available to the court is to announce that the rule that would lead to a wise decision will be applicable to future cases. But, in the case before the court, it would apply a rule that leads to a just result in that case (and applying that rule in the instant case, if it is a rule of the pre-existing law, could lead to a correct result in the instant case). Justice Hugo Black, the dissenting judge in the *Darrow* case, argued that this was the technique that the Supreme Court should employ.[126] It is much easier for a court to reach a just result in a case by applying a different rule than the rule that it desires to have applied to future cases when the rule that will be applied in the instant case is already a rule of the pre-existing law.

There is an element of unfairness in *ex post facto* (after the fact) incorrect decisions because the rule is being applied retroactively to conduct for which the rule was not applicable when the conduct was performed. In order to avoid the retroactivity, however, by employing the device of prospective overruling, the court creates potential unfairness in applying a different rule to present conduct than would be applied to future conduct.

Generally, a court should consider not changing a rule of the pre-existing law when its application to the instant case will result in an unjust decision. The *Darrow* case represents an example of a court creating a rule the application of which in the instant case does not lead to a just decision. The Supreme Court's decision in *Darrow*, therefore, if it created a new rule to govern the decision in the case before it, could result in an incorrect, unjust, but wise decision.

The Supreme Court recognized that it was holding the trustee liable even though the trustee made a profit for the trusts with the bond purchases he made. He had acquired no personal gain from the acts of the two employees. Johnson, the office manager, sometimes intervened between the seller of the bonds and the trusts as the potential buyer in order to make a profit for herself and Kulp in doing so. Darrow, however, did not profit from the activities of the two employees. The satisfaction of the judgment (the surcharge order) against him would have to be paid from his personal funds.

None of the justices on the Supreme Court suggested that the trustee had acted wrongfully. The Supreme Court's primary focus was, however, on the effects of its decision as a precedent:

> "These strict prohibitions would serve little purpose if the trustee were free to authorize others to do what he is forbidden. While there is no charge of it here, it is obvious that this would open up opportunities for devious dealings in the name of others that the trustee could not conduct on his own. The motives of men are too complex for equity to separate in the case of the trustee the motive of acquiring efficient help from motives of favoring help, for any reason at all or from authorization of counter favors later to come. We think that which the trustee had no right to do, he has no right to authorize, and that the transactions were as forbidden for benefit of others as they would have been on behalf of the trustee himself."[127]

The Supreme Court was worried about the difficulties of application of a rule that did not call for liability in the instant case:

> "But equity has sought to limit difficult and delicate fact-finding tasks concerning its own trustee by precluding such transactions for the reason that their effect is often difficult to trace, and the prohibition is not merely against

injuring the estate—it is against profiting out of the position of trust. That this has occurred, so far as the employees are concerned, is undenied."[128]

The reference to "equity" is to the equity courts which had been established in England to provide for certain specific kinds of cases, such as cases involving trusts.

It was clear that this was a large penalty to impose on a man who had made no personal profit and was not himself corrupt, but the majority opinion continued:

> "For all that appears, he was simply misled into thinking these persons indispensable, but he entered into an arrangement which courts cannot sanction unless they are to open the door to practices which would demoralize trusteeship and discredit bankruptcy administration."[129]

The Supreme Court concluded that it had to reach, in my terminology, an unjust, wise decision.

Justice Black, the dissenting justice, did not agree with the majority opinion that the Supreme Court had to reach an unjust, wise decision. He offered the Supreme Court a formula for reaching a just, wise decision. Justice Black in his dissenting opinion began by asserting that the decision was, once again in my terminology, incorrect: "This rule of trustee liability did not exist before today, as is shown by the fact that no statute or case is cited in support of the Court's decision."[130] Justice Black agreed with the majority opinion, however, that the rule that it was creating was a desirable rule.

He disagreed with the majority opinion about whether this rule should have been applied to this case:

> "Despite its novelty, there is much to be said in favor of such a rule for cases arising in the future. It seems to me, however, that there is no reason why the rule should be retroactively applied to this respondent [Darrow, the original defendant, who was the trustee when the fraud was

committed] when to do so is grossly unfair. Admittedly, the most that can be said against respondent is that he made an honest mistake which before today would not have subjected him to heavy financial penalty. Under these circumstances, if the new rule is to be announced by the Court, I think it should be given prospective application only."[131]

In summary, Justice Black asserted that the device of prospective overruling, or, more appropriately, in this case, avoiding *ex post facto* application of the new rule being created, should be used in order to avoid an unjust result in the instant case.

8.6 Concurring and dissenting opinions

Let us digress for one moment from the discussion of the unjust, wise decisions (*Conway* and *Darrow*) to mention two cases that are the converse of the retroactive decision. These cases also expand upon our consideration of the place of concurring and dissenting opinions in the development of the law.

Prospective application is the device used in two affirmative-action cases in which the prospective sunset of a legal rule is announced. In sharp contrast to Supreme Court Justices merely calling balls and strikes, let's look at two affirmative-action cases (these are cases in which a preference is given to African American students in admission to colleges to offset the disadvantages that they suffer from centuries of racial discrimination). There are multiple opinions in these two cases.

In the second case, there is the opinion for the Supreme Court by Justice O'Connor, a concurring opinion by Justice Ginsburg, an opinion concurring in part and dissenting in part by Justice Scalia, an opinion concurring in part and dissenting in part by Justice Thomas, a dissenting opinion by Justice Rehnquist, and a dissenting opinion by Justice Kennedy.

In the first affirmative-action decision, Chief Justice Rehnquist writes the opinion for the Court, Justice O'Connor writes a concurring opinion, Justice Thomas writes a concurring opinion, Justice Breyer writes an opinion concurring in the judgment, and Justices Stevens, Souter and Ginsburg all write separate dissenting opinions. This is not at all similar to the group of umpires at a baseball game conferring together to make a decision upon which they all agree.

The prospective sunset of a legal rule is announced by Justice Sandra Day O'Connor, in a concurring opinion in the first case: "We expect that 25 years from now, the use of racial preferences will no longer be necessary to further the interest approved today."[132] This statement is not binding on the Supreme Court because it is made in a concurring opinion. For a different perspective, consider Justice Thomas' statement in his concurring in part and dissenting in part opinion: "…I believe that the Law School's current use of race violates the Equal Protection Clause, and that the Constitution means the same thing today as it will in 300 months."[133]

It is very difficult to find a definitive legal rule in a decision with a multitude of different opinions. It is impossible to imagine a situation in a baseball game with four umpires disagreeing about whether a pitch is a ball or a strike. In any event, since umpires do not pronounce the reasons for their judgment calls, the umpires are making rational decisions in the sense that they are applying rules in a logical way, but they are not making rational, reasoned decisions, which is what judges do.

The *Black & White* case also illustrates another important aspect of judicial lawmaking. When judges write concurring and dissenting opinions, they are not in those opinions creating legal rules. Those opinions, however, allow for judges to be critical of legal rules that are being applied in the majority opinion. Judges use dissenting opinions not to create precedents but to criticize precedents, including the precedent that will be established by the majority opinion.

The judges writing concurring and dissenting opinions may be writing for the future or trying to convince a superior court to overrule the lower court or laying the groundwork for consideration of the case by the court *en banc* (consideration by a larger pane of judges) or trying to create a conflict in the circuits that will encourage the Supreme Court to grant certiorari and hear the case under consideration.[134] Sometimes the reasoning of the concurring or dissenting opinion ultimately becomes law when the precedent being criticized is overruled.[135]

8.7 Comparison of *Mosser v. Darrow* and *Conway v. Cutler Group*

I have included looking at both the *Darrow* case and the *Conway* cases because both decisions are unjust, wise decisions. They are very different, however, in two respects. I view the *Darrow* case as an incorrect, unjust, wise decision because there was no legal norm before this decision that allowed for trustees to be surcharged, so the decision was not consistent with pre-existing law and was, therefore, an incorrect decision. In the *Conway* case, there also was no prior case allowing for a subsequent purchaser of a house (a purchaser who is not the first purchaser/occupant) to be successful in a suit against the builder. Therefore, the decision for the builder was consistent with the pre-existing law and it was a correct decision.

The legal norm of the pre-existing law applicable in both cases was judicially established rather than established by legislation. There was no legal rule in the common law applicable to the *Darrow* case providing for liability of a trustee for the fraud committed by his employees when he received no personal benefit. In *Conway*, the implied warranty of habitability rule allowed for first purchasers of a house to prevail against the builder of the house for defects in the house, but Conway was not the first purchaser. The second difference between the two cases is that the U.S. Supreme Court in *Darrow* was quite willing to establish public policy, while the Pennsylvania Supreme Court in *Conway* was not. In both cases, they are the highest court in their legal system.

The *Darrow* case and the *Conway* case are similar in that in both cases an intermediate appellate court disagreed with the trial court. Then, the intermediate appellate court was reversed by an even higher court, which reinstated the decision of the trial court. The difference, though, is that the trial court in *Darrow* had made an incorrect decision and the trial court in *Conway* made the correct decision. Ultimately, then, *Darrow* is an incorrect, unjust wise decision and *Conway* is a correct, unjust wise decision.

I admit that the court's desire to reach a just decision should not blind it to the fact that its decision will be a precedent. The element of wisdom of the judicial decision is concerned with the desirability of the decision as a precedent (the consequences of the rule being created). Once it is clear that the pre-existing law is going to be changed, the problem before the judge is to make a change in the pre-existing law that will allow the decision to be a desirable precedent. In other words, the focus of the judge is to create a new rule that will have the most desirable social effects.

It may be argued that the *Darrow* case does not establish that the element of justice of the decision conflicted with the element of wisdom, but only that the Supreme Court failed to use an available acceptable remedy for the situation before the Supreme Court. The argument that the Supreme Court should consider a broader perspective than only a correct decision and should make a just decision could proceed as follows.

In any case in which the court would reach an unjust result if it applied a rule of the pre-existing law, and it wants to reach a just result, but it is concerned that the just result might be an unwise decision, the court can avoid the unwise decision and still reach a just result by creating a very narrow new rule that would allow for the just result. If the *ratio decidendi* of the case (the rule established by the decision), the new rule that is being created by the decision, is too broad, the court can create a very narrow rule (a rule with a relatively low degree of generality or applicability) that leads to a just result in the case before it.[136] This narrow rule will not result in an unwise decision since it will apply to very few future cases, and these cases will be very similar to the case in which the application of the rule led to a just decision.

In the *Webb* case (the case of the employee who was injured when he saved the life of his co-worker, which is my example of the just decision), the court created a narrow rule that allowed for a just decision. I cannot think of any reason why anyone would not also view this decision as a wise decision. The potential *ratio decidendi* of the *Webb* case is very narrow; the legal rule it established will not apply to many cases. The bottom line is that the court can base its decision on as narrow a ground as is expedient, so that there is no reason why a just decision cannot also be a wise decision by creating a legal rule which will not apply to cases that do not duplicate the peculiar and unusual factual situation in the case being decided.

After all, the argument could continue, it is important to notice that the law develops by creation of narrow legal rules as well as by creation of more general (broader) rules. And, frequently, after a narrow rule has shown that it is productive of just results, it can be expanded into a more general rule. For example, the rule of law that a plaintiff who is contributorily negligent cannot succeed in an accident case, even though the defendant's negligence was much greater than the plaintiff's negligence (which was very slight), often led to unjust results. An exception to this rule of contributory negligence was developed that eventually blossomed into the last clear chance rule.[137] This rule has been adopted in many common-law jurisdictions in which the law provides no mechanism for apportionment of responsibility and damages.

The last clear chance rule allows the plaintiff to recover when he has only been slightly negligent, and his negligent act occurs before the defendant's much greater negligent act and the defendant had the last opportunity to avoid the accident. This rule also allows the defendant to avoid liability if the plaintiff had the last clear chance to avoid the accident. In other words, the injustice of the results from application of the contributory negligence rule (which precludes recovery in an accident case even though the defendant has been negligent) are relaxed to allow recovery or a defense in a narrow type of case.

If, as in the *Darrow* case, the new rule is desirable, but it leads to an unjust result in the instant case, the court can, alternatively, follow Justice Black's suggestion. It can reach a just and wise result by prospective overruling of the precedent or changing the rule of the pre-existing law and thereby make a decision that is correct, just and wise. This is how the court can avoid a conflict between the just decision and the wise decision.

The approach that I am suggesting is less applicable to the situation in the *Conway* case because the Pennsylvania Supreme Court, like the trial court, is making a correct decision. As I will explain below, the correct decision is always presumptively justified. In this case, I think that the decision is unjust. In the *Elderkin* case, the Supreme Court referred to the unequal knowledge between the builder and the first purchaser of the house. In *Conway*, there also is unequal knowledge since the Conways did not know of the defect when they purchased the house and, presumably, the builder knew or should have known of the defect.

8.8 Landmark cases

In some cases, the element of justice is subordinate to the great significance of the rule being created. I would view the *Erie* case as such a situation. The change in the legal rule in the *Erie* case, however, did not itself lead to an unjust result because it appears as though Tompkins did not have a viable claim under Pennsylvania law, where the accident occurred. Ultimately, however, one may conclude that the just result, either by Pennsylvania common law or by federal common law, would require compensation for Tompkins. But the creation of the Erie Doctrine is so important and the effect of the decision on Tompkins is so much less significant that the consideration of the just decision is outweighed by the importance of the wise decision.

Another example of judicial activism would be *Brown v. Board of Education.*[138] The Supreme Court delayed imposing the remedy of ordering immediate desegregation of all schools in the United States, while granting relief to the brave children who brought the case. Unfortunately, even with the delayed implementation, the results have not been uniformly satisfactory regarding the integration of all schools in the country. My point in referring to this case is to use it as an example of a case in which the social consequences of the decision are of enormous weight. There also was potential harm in the disruption of all the schools in the United States (as well as the difficulty of management of such a massive change in the national system of education).

In *Donohue v. Stevenson*, the House of Lords decided that the manufacturer of ginger beer is liable to a customer when snails were found in one of its bottles.[139] In *Donohue*, as in *Brown v. Board of Education* and in *Erie*, the language employed by the respective courts is of a sufficiently broad nature that the cases are landmark cases in the law and are considered to have created new important legal rules.

In other cases, the court may be more concerned with reaching a correct decision than a just decision, especially when it views the applicable legal rule of the pre-existing law as a desirable rule.[140] You could conclude that Judge Gavin was so inclined in making his decision in the *O'Brien* case (this is the first case I discussed in which the employee wanted to compete with his former employer, and it is my example of a correct decision). One may also view the decision in Conway as the Supreme Court exercising justifiable caution in leaving the issue to the legislature to resolve.

8.9 The two-level method

The cases that I have discussed in the previous section reflect a variety of judicial techniques that can be employed to achieve desirable results in deciding lawsuits. The ability to employ these techniques relates to the craftsmanship of the individual judge (or body of judges in cases heard by a panel of judges). In every case, the judge can elect to apply the pre-existing law. In some cases, it is more prudent to create a new narrow legal rule or a narrow exception to a rule. In other cases, the judge can be more creative, and she can develop a new legal rule of a more general nature. But the problem remains of determining when a more general rule will be more desirable than a less general rule. This is where the great judges outshine the good judges, where the judicial craft is most noticeable.

Richard A. Wasserstrom, a professor of law at Stanford University, presents in *The Judicial Decision*, one of the best descriptions of a decision-making method that I have read. Wasserstrom argues that consideration of the utility of legal rules will emphasize the fact that decisions are precedents, and, as precedents, they have effects upon the society and the courts should consider these effects in reaching their decisions.[141]

He presents a theory of a two-level process of legal justification: "It is a two-level procedure of legal justification in which courts are to justify their decisions by appealing to legal rules, and in which they are to justify their legal rules by appealing to the principles of utility."[142] Wasserstrom compares his theory to the "equitable theory of justification." The equitable theory would justify a decision if and only if it produces more satisfaction and a minimum of dissatisfaction to the litigants. He asserts that his two-level theory is superior to the equitable theory because his theory considers not only the litigants but also the social effects of the decision on the society.

The equitable theory emphasizes the unique facts of each case. In this respect, it is similar to Jerome N. Frank's legal philosophy of focusing on the facts of the cases and helps ensure that the decisions will be just decisions. Near the end of his book, Wasserstrom seems to incorporate justice (or equity) into his two-level procedure: "The two-level procedure is like the equitable decision procedure in its requirement that considerations of justice or utility be relevant to the justification of decisions."[143] It is this statement that planted the seed for the theory of the three elements of the judicial decision: correct, just and wise.

8.10 Presumptive justification of the correct decision

Creative positivism, the legal theory that I am proposing, accepts the presumptive justification of the correct decision supplemented by the potential justification of justice and wisdom in making judicial decisions. The correct decision is always presumptively justified because of the obligatory nature of the law (the legal rules of the pre-existing law that should in the usual case be applied to make the correct decision). The making of the judicial decision, however, includes considering more than the law because a court of law is also a court of justice and by its decisions it is creating precedents for the deciding of future cases.

Wasserstrom outlines a two-level process of first finding what the correct decision would be and then justifying either that correct decision or an alternative decision that satisfies the standard of utility. I am suggesting, instead, that the correct decision is presumptively justified, but the judge should also consider whether a just and/or a wise decision would be a preferable decision (a good decision) rather than the correct decision. When thinking about the just and/or wise decision, the judge may conclude that the correct decision is also the just and/or wise decision.

Before I describe my theory of justification of the correct, just and wise decisions, which I call creative positivism, I want to put my theory in an historical context (which is the subject of *The Judge and the*

Philosopher). My theory is the potential successor to theories that have come before it. The traditional theory and its ultimate successor, legal positivism, lend support to the correct decision. The American Legal Realists, especially Jerome Frank and Karl Llewellyn, destroyed the primacy of the correct decision and allowed us to recognize expansion of the sources of judicial decisions to include what I have called justice and wisdom (the latter being the consideration of the consequences of the decision as a precedent). H.L.A. Hart, the leading legal positivist who presented the format for how the legal system should be viewed, put legal rules into the context of the legal system and the legal system he describes, with its primary and secondary rules, allows us to separate the correct decision from the incorrect decision.

I then borrowed and modified Richard Wasserstrom's two-level theory of justification into a three-element theory of presumptive justification of correctness, supplemented by consideration of justice and wisdom. At this point, I want to revisit the six cases. I will then present a brief introduction to creative positivism. In the final chapter, I will summarize the reasons why judges are not like umpires.

9.
REVISTING THE SIX CASES

While my focus is not on what judges actually do, I recognize that a legal theory to be acceptable has to bear some relationship to what is really happening in the legal world. For this reason, I wanted to present actual cases to demonstrate that the theory that I am presenting, which I call creative positivism, has some relevance to what judges do. Creative positivism is my attempt to provide the "semantics of judicial decision-making"—a vocabulary for the review, analysis and discussion about particular decisions. There are customary norms that govern where, when and how judicial decisions are made, and, in addition, who makes them (who are the judges and what is their authority). I discuss the customary norms in *The Judge and the President*.

The vocabulary that I am proposing is that decisions should be considered from the perspective of whether they are correct, just and/or wise. While the correct decision itself, in order to be justified, does not involve evaluation, the issue of whether the correct decision is the best decision is an evaluative process. These three elements are the evaluative standards that may be employed in looking at the six cases that I have outlined and now want to review.

9.1 *O'Brien v. Desco Steel Corp.*

O'Brien v. Desco Steel Corp., in Chapter Two, is my example of a correct decision. This is the case in which the employee who signed a non-compete agreement left his job and wanted to compete with his former employer. While Judge Gavin mentions morals and equity, he decides to disregard those standards and to make the correct decision. The correct decision may be an immoral and an unethical decision. In making the correct decision, Judge Gavin believes that he is deciding the case by applying pre-existing law. He finds the law to apply to decide the case rather than create a new law.

We generally call a decision "correct" if it is consistent with the law that was in existence before the decision is reached and the decision does not change the legal rule being applied to make the decision. Therefore, the judge in making a correct decision is discovering the law that, if applied, will determine the outcome in the case. The focus of the judge is on consistency with the pre-existing law available when the decision is made.

While Judge Gavin is not changing the law when he makes his decision, each individual published case, to a limited extent and with some exceptions, does affect the law. The pre-existing law for the next case includes this decision. The law is constantly evolving, moving, flexing, stretching, expanding and contracting. This is how the law retains flexibility. Most cases are micro, though a few rare cases are macro in effect. Nevertheless, and this is essential, there is sufficient certainty in the law and in the application of the law for it to be stable and determinate.

The *O'Brien* case involves interpretation of a contract. Contract law has been developed primarily by cases being decided by courts. The type of case that the judge is considering has an impact upon the use of elements other than the law. In areas of the law where predictability of judicial decisions is paramount, such as interpreting contracts that were written with the understanding that the contract may eventually be interpreted in a court of law, predictability of how the contract will be interpreted is the foundation for the drafting of the contract. Judges consider this factor in making their decision.

In *O'Brien v. Desco Steel Corp.*, we have two parties who are unequal in many respects. Desco is a successful, profitable company with a long record of service to its customers. O'Brien is a young man who came to Desco with no experience in the industry. He received on-the-job training, and he had access to Desco's customers and suppliers. He obviously has talent because he was able to produce sales that allowed him to receive substantial compensation in the form of commissions that he earned.

O'Brien, reading between the lines of Judge Gavin's opinion, may be viewed as having some character flaws. He lacks credibility, steals the customer list and is ungrateful for the opportunity and training he had received. But he is entitled to earn income for his work, and he has developed a skill set that enables him to be successful in the same business environment as that of Desco. He did, however, sign the non-compete agreement, he had the opportunity to have it reviewed by a lawyer and he did read it before signing it.

Desco paid O'Brien $500 for agreeing not to compete. O'Brien argues that this is inadequate consideration for the promise he made, but he did not ask for a larger payment. Judge Gavin does not decide the case on the basis that the agreement is unenforceable by reason of inadequate consideration. One could argue that the payment of $500 is not adequate consideration for someone agreeing not to compete for one year and thereby losing a six-figure income for that year.

Judge Gavin considers whether there is economic necessity for Desco to be protected from competition by O'Brien. Due to Desco's economic strength and years of experience in the industry, Judge Gavin concludes that there is no economic necessity for the limitation on competition because O'Brien lacks financial capital to generate business that would create substantial harm to Desco's revenue.

In light of these facts, is the decision in favor of O'Brien a just decision? Let's assume that it is. What then are the factors in the case that lead to this conclusion?

When one is seeking relief, there must be a basis for granting them the benefits they are requesting. In this case, the harm to O'Brien of denying him the opportunity to ply his trade is substantially greater than the harm to Desco of having O'Brien as a competitor. The difference in moral conduct is clearly a factor for deciding the case in favor of Desco, but Judge Gavin does not base his decision on the comparative moral character of the parties (in some cases, this would be highly significant, such as in a custody of children case).

Therefore, we may conclude that justice requires that the party suffering the burden must be significantly harmed, that the party receiving the benefit has to have a real stake in getting the benefit (in this case, by earning income by being allowed to compete) and that weighing the relative benefits and burdens tips the scale in this case to the plaintiff O'Brien.

But Judge Gavin is obviously troubled that the judgment for O'Brien might be immoral or unequitable. He does not expand upon his reasons for this reaction to the arguments of the parties. O'Brien clearly had acted in ways that could be regarded as immoral or unethical and Desco had not done anything wrong. The immorality in O'Brien's conduct, and maybe his character, is not directly pertinent to the issue framed by Judge Gavin. Therefore, he makes the correct decision in applying the relevant legal norms.

One could argue that this result is unjust to Desco. The company invested in O'Brien by training him. Now, he would be competing with the company. Once again, depriving O'Brien of the opportunity to operate in the industry of selling rebar is a greater imposition than the loss that Desco would suffer. So, another conclusion from this case could be that justice is always relative, specific situation based and reflective of the impact on the parties of the decision.

I interviewed Judge Gavin in order to discuss with him my theory of the three elements. I specifically asked him if he ever had to make a decision that challenged his moral views. He said that he personally disapproves of abortion. Yet, he granted a petition for a prisoner who wanted an abortion because he thought that the law required that he grant the request, notwithstanding his personal beliefs. Similarly, but not necessarily challenging his personal moral standards, he decided the *O'Brien* case in favor of O'Brien even though he (Judge Gavin) felt that the result may not conform to moral and equitable norms (see my notes from my interview of Judge Gavin in Appendix A).

In considering whether the decision for O'Brien is a wise decision, it could be argued that any decision that promotes competition is consistent with the capitalistic economy that flourishes in the U.S. But one could also argue that a decision in favor of Desco would encourage companies to invest in training employees who have no experience in the industry in which they will be working. Neither of these positions appears to have influenced Judge Gavin. He does consider economics when he finds that there is no economic necessity for Desco to be protected from competition from O'Brien. I would consider the decision to be a wise decision because it encourages competition which will ultimately result in lower prices for the items being constructed by using the rebar being sold.

9.2 *Cincinnati Insurance Co v. Flannery Electric Motor Service, Inc.*

In the *Cincinnati* cases (Chapter Four), the federal court, using the Erie Doctrine promulgated in the *Erie* case discussed in Chapter Six, looked to Indiana law and did not read the tea leaves accurately. Flannery was attempting to establish that Cincinnati Insurance Co. was obligated to provide insurance coverage when the EPA wanted to extract the cost for environmental remediation. The pollution was caused by the company that Flannery was using for the disposal of old equipment.

Flannery would have had insurance coverage if the case had been tried in the Indiana state courts, but he lost the case in the federal system. Looking at this case through the lens of the three elements that I am proposing that may be applied in evaluating the judicial decision, the decision in the *Cincinnati 1* case was incorrect, unjust and unwise. The decision in accordance with the Erie Doctrine did reflect an attempt to decide the case based upon the pre-existing law without any consideration of a just or wise result.

The *Cincinnati* case involves interpretation of an insurance contract. Insurance contracts are very confusing. They usually have many pages of tight print, then many pages of exclusions, and then additional pages of amendments to the exclusions that qualify or expand the exclusions, which in turn qualify or reduce the extend of insurance coverage. Because of the way insurance companies draft their contracts, courts must constrain insurance companies from engaging in misleading practices. The insurance policies deceive parties who believe that they are purchasing insurance coverage when the contract, as written, does not provide the insurance coverage that the purchaser of the insurance expects to receive.

In addition, it is of great benefit to the society that environmental remediation be undertaken. Flannery thought it had purchased insurance that would protect it from being accused of environmental pollution and would cover the cost of remediation of the pollution. The federal courts made a mistake in their prediction of what the Indiana courts would decide in the interpretation of the insurance contract. For these reasons, I conclude that *Cincinnati 1* was an incorrect and unjust decision. It may also be an unwise decision because it does not promote a clean environment, though as I will explain below, this may be an unfair criticism.

As I mentioned in Chapter Four, this case illustrates that a judicial decision can be both incorrect and still be binding upon the parties. The decision in *Cincinnati 1*, however, is not authoritative for the

Indiana legal system. Also, even though incorrect, the decision is authorized because it is based upon the Erie Doctrine. Consideration of whether this is a wise decision is irrelevant because the decision is not an authoritative precedent for the next case in federal court considering this type of insurance policy. The federal court would apply Indiana law and Indiana law after the decision in *Cincinnati 1* provides for insurance coverage.

The concept of the incorrect decision by mistake must be understood for the correct decision to be plausible. There cannot be incorrect decisions without there also being correct decisions. In this manner, the incorrect decision and the correct decision are coupled so that neither can exist without the other.

9.3 *Webb v. McGowin*

In the *Webb* case, which was discussed in Chapter Five, the court disregarded the pre-existing law and found for Webb, making a just decision. This is the case in which Webb suffered an injury that resulted in his being incapable of working when he jumped off the second floor, redirected the wooden block and saved McGowin's life. For doing so, McGowin promised to pay Webb $15 every two weeks for the rest of Webb's life.

Webb saved McGowin from serious injury or possible death and, in doing so, suffered a substantial injury. He was no longer able to work. McGowin, obviously feeling gratitude toward Webb, made the promise to pay him biweekly for the rest of Webb's life. When McGowin died, without making any provision for continuation of the biweekly payments, the executors of his estate discontinued making the payments.

According to the applicable legal norms of the pre-existing law, McGowin's promise lacked adequate consideration and was not a legally binding promise. The court, however, decided that Webb was entitled to continuation of the biweekly payments.

Webb suffered a significant injury. McGowin, because of Webb's willingness to risk injury himself, was not injured. But McGowin had not asked Webb to take any action. He had not promised Webb anything before Webb acted. McGowin, however, did promise to make the biweekly payments after the incident occurred.

There is a clear distinction between obligation and charity—the former being something that one must do, and the latter is something that one does not have to do but wants to do because it is the right thing to do. Prior to the decision in the *Webb* case, there was no basis in the law or reason why the promise that McGowin made would be regarded as a legally binding promise rather than a charitable non-binding gesture.

McGowin's promise was the just thing for him to do. Ask yourself these questions. When McGowin made the promise, did he think that he was committing himself to a legally binding duty? If he did, why did he not include this obligation in his will so that it would survive his death and provide for Webb to receive the biweekly checks after he died? Would your answer be different if McGowin had a meager estate, and his heirs would receive very little after Webb was paid? If McGowin was able to provide substantial assets for his heirs and the $15 every two weeks did not really have any material impact on their quality of life, would that affect your reasoning about the legal nature of McGowin's promise?

These last two questions are irrelevant in determining what the correct decision would be. What is relevant is whether McGowin wanted to commit himself to doing what was the right thing to do and he made his promise and honored it during his lifetime. We must assume that he wanted and expected his heirs to fulfill his promise after his death. When you frame the issue this way, the decision in this case merely results in McGowin's wishes being honored and Webb's expectations being realized.

From the point of view of Webb, who made the sacrifice to his own health in order to give a significant and substantial benefit to McGowin, the result in the case is clearly just. It is not only a charitable act on McGowin's part but requiring that the payments be made to Webb is the honoring of McGowin's clear intention.

The conclusion about justice that I draw from the *Webb* decision is that, if the parties in the case believe a particular result will be just, the judgment of the court that fulfills their expectations is very likely to be the just decision. Justice is not only a legal concept, but it is also a moral concept. Morality requires that we act in a just way. The just act is likely to be the moral act. Law may sometimes overlap with morality and require the same act that morality requires. In some cases, the moral act will be legally neutral. Ensuring that McGowin's promise was honored required that the court make the just decision. I will discuss the interaction between moral rules and legal rules in *The Judge and the Philosopher*.

My evaluation of the *Webb* case is that it is an incorrect decision that was reached in order to provide for a just decision. If this factual situation was presented in the twenty-first century, it would be a workman's compensation case. Webb would be suing his employer who would have been required by state law to carry workmen's compensation insurance. The case would have been started in an administrative procedure rather than in a trial court.

Workmen's compensation law is based upon statutes that create an administrative process to decide cases involving the compensation of injured employees. If the employee disagrees with the result in the administrative process, an appeal may be filed in court. There are regulations that have been adopted to implement the statute and provide for the administrative procedure. There are also regulations, both at the state level and the federal level, stipulating norms that are designed to provide for employee safety.

The question of whether the decision in the *Webb* case qualifies as the wise decision is insignificant because of the narrowness of the legal rule created in the decision. This legal rule will apply only in very rare cases.

9.4 *Erie Railroad Co. v. Tompkins*

The U.S. Supreme Court, in the *Erie* case in Chapter Six, overruled *Swift v. Tyson*. The *Swift* case was an almost one-hundred-year established precedent. In *Erie*, the Supreme Court discarded thousands of precedents based upon federal common law that had been used in federal court in diversity-of-citizenship cases and mandated a new source of law to be used to decide those cases. This is the case in which a swinging railroad car door struck Tompkins as he was walking on a pathway next to the railroad tracks. The decision is clearly not a correct decision since the pre-existing law required that federal law be applied and Tompkins had prevailed in the District Court when the jury, applying federal law, reached a verdict for him.

My analysis regarding justice is completely different when we consider the *Erie* case. Tompkins would have lost in the Pennsylvania courts where Pennsylvania law would be applied. He elected to go to federal court, and he also lost in that court. You could argue that Pennsylvania law was unjust, but I think that there is some justification for the Pennsylvania legal norms.

Tompkins made the decision to walk next to the track. He ignored the train's horn and he saw the train's lights. Pennsylvania law recognizes a difference between crossing the tracks and walking next to them. Sometimes you must cross the tracks to get to your destination. You do not have to walk next to the tracks and Tompkins could have easily walked on the street. He was clearly a trespasser if Pennsylvania law was applied and he, therefore, would not have prevailed in the Pennsylvania courts.

The *Erie* decision is a wise decision because the policy basis for the decision is a sound policy. In contrast to the U.S. Supreme Court demonstrating no reluctance to make this policy decision, the Pennsylvania Supreme Court in the next case we will consider ducked the policy decision and made the correct decision.

9.5 *Conway v. Cutler Group*

The *Conway* case presents the issue of whether the purchaser who is not the first purchaser of a house should bear the burden of faulty craftsmanship when the house he has purchased was built with defects. Alternatively, the builder of the house could be liable for the defects. If you agree that the builder should be liable since it was his negligence that caused the problem, are there any limits to this liability? Does it end after 5 years, 10 years or 20 years? Does it extend to the 3rd, 6th or 10th purchaser of the house? Does it have any monetary limits? Should repair of the defects be covered by insurance required to be purchased by either the builder or the purchaser of the house?

Since these are difficult questions to answer, the trial court and the Supreme Court viewed the *Conway* case as calling for legislative action regarding the structuring of the implied warranty of habitability. I conclude that this decision for Cutler Group was a correct and wise decision because the judicially created implied warranty of habitability did not protect purchasers who did not enter into a contract with the builder to buy the house. The questions that I have raised in the prior paragraph present difficult issues. It is quite plausible to maintain, however, that the courts have the responsibility to determine the parameters of the implied warranty of habitability since the courts created the implied warranty.

The difference among the three decisions in the *Conway* case was based upon whether the court should or should not change the legal rule that would be applied to decide the case. All the judges considering the case at the three levels of the judicial hierarchy were operating with the same understanding of what the pre-existing law was. All three decisions, in addition, were authorized, authoritative and binding when the decisions were made, even though the results of the decisions were conflicting. Ultimately, the law is what the highest court says it is subject to customary norms about the authoritativeness of judicial decisions. The issue in the three efforts to decide the case was not "what is the law" but, instead, whether the law should be modified.

The three decisions, then, reflect the insight inherent in H.L.A. Hart's rule of recognition. There was common agreement among these judges (one judge in the trial court; multiple judges in both the intermediate appellate court and the highest court) about where to find the applicable law, how to find the applicable law and what the applicable law was. Hart bases his rule of recognition on this general agreement among judicial officials of how to find the applicable law.

Contrary to Ronald Dworkin's approach that presupposes that the differences in the three decisions is a difference about how the law will be interpreted, all the judges interpreted the applicable law to be that the basic legal rule established in the *Elderkin* case applied only to first-time buyer/occupants. The issue in the *Conway* case was whether that legal rule should be modified and not a disagreement about the legal rule itself or how it should be interpreted.

I view the decision of the Pennsylvania Supreme Court in the *Conway* case as a correct, unjust and wise decision. It is correct because it applied the pre-existing law. It is a wise decision because the policy issues are so complex that the legislature is more equipped to resolve them than the courts. It is unjust because Conway had no way of knowing that there were defects when he bought the house, and the builder of the house should have known about the defects.

9.6 *Mosser v. Darrow*

Next, let's consider *Mosser v. Darrow*. Darrow was surcharged for the self-serving acts of the two employees of the trusts. He received no personal benefit from their acts. The trusts were well-managed by him and the two employees, though the trusts could have received more income if the two employees were not self-dealing for their own account.

Prior to the decision in this case, no trustee in a bankruptcy proceeding had ever been surcharged for the fraudulent acts of employees of the company involved in the bankruptcy proceedings. Moreover, the trustee himself, Darrow, received no benefit. The Supreme Court wanted to put future trustees on notice that they would be held to be responsible for the fraudulent acts of the employees of the bankrupt company whom they hire. It would be expedient, then, for the court to not look into what possible benefit the trustee might receive and impose a blanket general rule of virtually strict liability (liability without consideration of the specific circumstances in the case).

Was applying the rule of strict liability to Darrow, however, fair to him? He had no notice that he might be personally liable for the acts of the two employees. The bankruptcy court had approved his hiring of the two employees. Darrow allowed them to trade in the bonds for their own account, which was something they had always done. This was a condition that they had insisted upon in order to continue to manage the two trusts. He also could not have anticipated that he might be liable for their actions.

Justice incorporates the element of fairness. It was not fair for the trusts and the creditors of the trusts to lose the profit that the trusts could have made if the employees had acted in the best interests of the trusts. It is the two employees who should have been surcharged or required to make restitution rather than Darrow being surcharged, when Darrow acted in good faith and received no personal benefit and had no notice that he could be held to be liable for the acts of the two employees. In short, I agree with the dissenting opinion that this was a good opportunity for pronouncing a rule to apply to future cases but not apply it to the instant case. Applying the rule to Darrow was unfair because it was *ex post facto* (retroactive).[144]

Each of these six cases involves a somewhat different theory of justice. Justice is a multi-faceted concept that is deeply fact-driven and completely individual-party relevant. Considering whether a decision is just or unjust requires drilling down into the specific facts, the intentions of the parties, the relative benefits and burdens to be received by the parties, the fairness and equality involved in the specific case and many other factors. Justice is highly individualistic and case-specific in a way that general rule-application cannot emulate. Courts apply general rules, but they also dispense justice, and the correct decision may not be the just decision. In fact, in some cases, such as in the *Darrow* case, the incorrect decision is not the just decision.

Hart's rule of change, another of his secondary rules in his legal theory, is demonstrated by the U.S. Supreme Court in the *Darrow* case changing the pre-existing law to create a new legal rule. In fact, the Supreme Court created a new cause of action that did not exist before this decision and that established that trustees could be surcharged for the fraud of the employees that they hired to manage the bankrupt estate. This new rule was based upon a legal principle (the legal principle is that the bankrupt entity and its creditors should not suffer the loss that is the result of the fraudulent acts of its employees). I agree with Hart that the law consists of the legal rules but not necessarily legal principles. Principles are not part of the law, but they are relevant to changes made to the law. I will discuss the relationship of legal principles and legal rules in *The Judge and the Philosopher*.

The operating principle that the Supreme Court looked to in order to create the new legal rule is that the courts are not equipped to decide when their trustees would or would not receive a benefit when employees they hired are dishonest. Darrow was held to be liable for the fraudulent acts of the employees even though he did not receive a benefit. The Darrow case is not a correct decision because it was not made by applying a rule of the pre-existing law.

You cannot apply a principle to arrive at a correct decision. For a correct decision, you must apply a legal rule of the pre-existing law. It follows, then, that the correct decision is consistent with Hart's rule of recognition, while the incorrect decision is supported by his rule of change.

The legal system reflects many policies. These policies may conflict with each other. The laws themselves, however, never conflict in the sense that disputes must be resolved, correct decisions are presumptively justified, and correct decisions are made by applying the pre-existing law. If there is a potential conflict in the legal norms, it is resolved by applying the legal norm that is most applicable. There is always a potential legal norm to apply to resolve every dispute because the law is coherent, comprehensive, complete and consistent so that, in making the judicial decision, the decision necessarily eliminates any potential conflict. There is never a tie; every case will result in a decision.

Policies will be a factor in the legal system in many ways, though policies may conflict with each other. The element of the wise decision presupposes that there is a best decision. The best decision may be an alternate source decision (the just decision and/or the wise decision). In order to make the wise decision, policies must be evaluated. For the wise decision to be compared to the correct decision, the legal norm that would result in the correct decision has to be evaluated. The correct decision is the decision that would be made by applying pre-existing law with no requirement of evaluation of the legal norm to be applied to do so.

There are policies embedded in the law (in the legal norms). There are also policies inherent in the legal system. These are all public policies. These policies, from these multiple sources, could conflict. The wise decision must resolve that conflict, by selecting from among the policies. The decision to avoid making the policy decision (as in the *Conway* case in Chapter Seven) is itself the implementation of a policy, to wit, the policy to leave policy decisions to the legislature. In the *Elderkin* case (also in Chapter Seven), the decision was made to adopt a policy to protect home purchasers who had less bargaining power and knowledge than home builders, by creating the implied warranty of habitability. Thus, the Pennsylvania Supreme Court in the *Elderkin* case created a legal norm, which the Supreme Court declined to modify but which it left intact in the *Conway* case.

While it is beyond the scope of this book, this application of the rule of change presents an issue that Hart does not discuss. I mentioned Hart's rule of recognition above. In the *Darrow* case, as in the *Conway* case, the basic issue was not about what the law was. There was no rule in the pre-existing law in the *Darrow* case providing for a surcharge. When the just decision or the wise decision is made, and it is not a correct decision, the rule of change overrules the rule of recognition (the legal norm provided pursuant to the rule of recognition is not applied). Hart's theory does not accommodate or explain this conflict between the two secondary rules.

The judge may make the correct decision without evaluating whether the legal rule being applied is a just or unjust rule or a wise or unwise rule. Similarly, the judge may not evaluate whether the decision being made, while it is a correct decision, is the best decision that could be made. When the judge wants to evaluate the decision being made, he will consider whether the decision is a just decision or a wise decision. There is, however, also potential conflict between the just decision and the wise decision.

Finally, the decision in the *Darrow* case is an incorrect, unjust and wise decision. It is incorrect because there was no rule in the pre-existing law providing for a surcharge. It is unjust because applying the rule that the Supreme Court created to Darrow was unfair because Darrow could not anticipate that he would be liable for the fraudulent acts of the two employees. It is a wise decision because there must be rules in regard to the responsibilities of trustees and it makes sense for the rule to provide for liability if the bankrupt estate is defrauded. Trustees can purchase fiduciary insurance to protect the bankrupt estate from fraud by employees.

9.7 The just decision v. the wise decision

Sometimes, when the just decision is made, the consequences are less significant because the judge makes it clear that he considers the instant case to be an unusual or extraordinary case and he creates a narrow rule to apply in the instant case that will not affect many future cases. A good example would be the decision in the *Webb* case.

Justice Black, in his dissenting opinion in the *Darrow* case, had no objection to the rule that the majority wanted to create, but he urged that the rule not be applied to *Darrow*. If that suggestion had been accepted, it would have resulted in a just decision. As Karl Llewellyn, one of the American Legal Realists, notes, it is the judge's duty to decide the case based upon a rule of law, but not necessarily a rule of law that can be applied to all seemingly like cases.[145]

It is also possible that the consequences of the wise decision may be so favorable that the effect upon the parties in the case becomes very much secondary or even non-existent as a factor in evaluating the decision. For example, in the *Erie* case, because it was a groundbreaking, rule-changing and system-changing blockbuster decision, the effect on Tompkins and even on Erie Railroad was much less important than the substantial change in public policy.

I would characterize the *Darrow* case as another example of the wise decision overwhelming the just decision and the correct decision. The focus of the Supreme Court was on establishing a workable legal rule for the future that would control trustees, be easily administered and protect creditors and the bankrupt entity. The goal was to establish a clear rule that would eliminate uncertainty and be dogmatic regarding what activities would be permissible in the future regulation of trustees.

Darrow, who did nothing wrong from a moral or ethical point of view, but who did make a mistake, was the victim of the wise decision.

In the case, the Pennsylvania Supreme Court refused to extend the implied warranty of habitability, which this court had created. For reasons that are not clearly presented, the Supreme Court viewed the expansion of the implied warranty of habitability as too involved with public policy to allow for an extension of the warranty—the Supreme Court was at the end of its self-imposed law-creation capacity, and it made the correct decision. The decision reflects customary norms that regulate judicial activism in creating law. The correct decision in the *Conway* case may have been the wise decision but it was not the just decision.

Between the decision of the trial court and the decision of the Supreme Court in the *Conway* case, there was a decision by the Superior Court. The Superior Court did not want to affirm the decision of the trial court and it reversed that decision, only to be reversed in turn by the Supreme Court.

A reversal by an appellate court is not a penalty; it is just a reversal. It changes the result in the case. The Superior Court made an incorrect, just and unwise decision when it decided in favor of the Conway family. The Supreme Court, then, agreed with the trial court and made a correct, unjust and wise decision.

I never had the opportunity to discuss the Conway case with Hart. I wonder how he would characterize the decision of the Superior Court. This is not a case of a gap in the law. The law is clear, so it is not an example of open texture. Finally, I do not think that either the decision in *Elderkin*, which established the implied warranty of habitability, or the decision in *Conway* can really be characterized as a core case (in *Elderkin*, there was no rule of the pre-existing law to be interpreted when the Supreme Court created an entirely new rule).

The level of court is obviously a factor in how much leeway the court has to change the law. An interesting aspect of the *Conway* case is that, while the Supreme Court, the highest of the three courts that heard this case, was unwilling to extend the legal norm it had established in the *Elderkin* case, the Superior Court voted to do so. This then defies the principle that the higher the court in the judicial hierarchy the more likely the court is to reach for the just decision or the wise decision. In this instance, the highest court agreed with the trial court that the correct decision should be made, reversing the intermediate appellate court that wanted to make either the just decision or the wise decision or both. It is also important to note that the Superior Court was not reversed because it had made an incorrect decision; it was reversed because the Supreme Court wanted to make a correct decision rather than to consider what the wise decision would be.

9.8 The obligation to make the correct decision

This section is about the beating heart of creative positivism. Some of the American Legal Realists endorsed the theory that there is no such thing as the correct decision because law is too indeterminate to allow for finding and applying the legal rules. Some legal theorists will argue that there is no correct decision in all cases or in some cases. The law, however, is comprehensive and complete and I have contended that there are no gaps in the law. I will discuss the issue of gaps in *The Judge and the Philosopher*.

Ever since *The Concept of Law* was published by Hart in 1961, most legal positivists believe that judges are obligated to make the correct decision. Creative positivism advances the theory that the correct decision is presumptively justified. You may extend that view to refer to making the correct decision as an obligation, but this then requires that you explain what it means to have such an obligation.

It is not logical to argue that there can be more than one correct decision. For example, you cannot argue that a decision for either Conway or for Cutler Group can both be a correct decision. That position is illogical because the pre-existing law must be authoritative to be effective.

I can cite many cases that are correct decisions and some cases in which the decision that was made was not a correct decision. But the bottom line is that either a decision for Conway or a decision for Cutler Group is the correct decision. Since, prior to the *Conway* case, there was never a case in Pennsylvania in which the purchaser of a home could prevail against a builder who was not the seller of the home (there are inapplicable exceptions to this proposition), I conclude that Conway could not make out a cause of action against the Cutler Group. Since Conway has no cause of action, a decision in favor of Conway would not be the correct decision and a decision in favor of the Cutler Group would be the correct decision.

Consequently, when the Court of Common Pleas decided in favor of the Cutler Group, this was a correct decision. Then, the Superior Court reversed that result and decided for Conway. I will repeat this point because of its importance. The Superior Court did not reverse the trial court because the judges in the Superior Court thought that the pre-existing law did provide a cause of action. They did not find an existing legal rule that the trial court missed or conclude that the trial court had made a mistake regarding what the pre-existing law was. Instead, they decided that the implied warranty of habitability should be extended to include a cause of action for the second purchaser against the original builder.

The Cutler Group took an appeal to the Supreme Court. The Cutler Group, once again, made the same argument in the Supreme Court that they had made in the trial court and in the Superior Court. They argued that the implied warranty of habitability should not be extended, or, if it is to be extended, it should be by the legislature and not by the courts. The Supreme Court, like the Superior Court, did not conclude that the inferior court had applied the wrong rule of the pre-existing law. Instead, the Supreme Court opted for applying the pre-existing law and making the correct decision.

All three courts in the *Conway* case, and their multiple judges, agreed on what the correct decision would be. The issue for all three courts and their multiple judges was whether the legal rule should be extended in order to make a just decision (and, maybe, a wise decision), even though such a decision would not be a correct decision. This, then, is a prime example of courts deciding which element of the three elements should prevail.

None of the judges involved in the various phases of the *Conway* case acted illegally. All the judges performed their duties in accordance with their sworn responsibility to act in a professional manner in accordance with their oath of office. None of these judges made a mistake about law-ascertainment. I would suggest that the *Conway* case is a prime example of how the three elements are part of decision-making and are workable criteria for analyzing decisions after they are made.

10.
INTRODUCTION TO CREATIVE POSITIVISM

Legal philosophy starts with the law. To arrive at an understanding of law and its place in a modern society, let's begin with Justice Brandeis' view, described in Chapter Six when we considered *Erie Railroad Co. v. Tompkins*. Justice Brandeis declared that law consists of the statutes, the precedents and customs having the force of law.[146] Based upon Hart's rule of recognition, for the United States, I would add to Brandeis' list the written Constitution (in England, it would be the documents that are part of the constitutional framework), and written and unwritten constitutional principles (which are also part of the Constitution). I would also add laws created by the Executive Branch of the government, administrative agencies and quasi-judicial boards.

The law itself is not subject to any particular notion of justice. There is no evaluation of individual laws to qualify as part of the law in regard to their effectiveness, acceptability or morality. In short, the law is the law, which consists of the legal rules derived from the Constitution, statutes, precedents and customs with the force of law.[147] A law is the legal rule derived from the aforementioned sources of the law.

Hart's system of primary rules and secondary rules (which I briefly described in Section 2.4) helps in describing the bare bones of a legal system in a mature democratic society. The legal system includes not only the law but all of the other operational aspects of how laws are created and applied and the practices of the officials (the law-actors) who have the responsibility for creating laws and/or applying them.

The judicial decision will be a correct or an incorrect decision regardless of whether one believes the decision is a good or a bad decision (good or bad means that you approve or disapprove of the decision). The judge (and the critic) should start with the correct decision because the correct decision is presumptively justified in all cases.

Law is by its nature obligatory. Citizens are obligated to obey the law in their own conduct. Judges and other officials take an oath to perform their roles as legal officials in accordance with the law. If you go to the clerk who issues marriage licenses, and you meet the criteria that are relevant for obtaining a marriage license, the clerk has no discretion. He is obligated to issue the license, even if he disagrees with the relevant legal norms. He must give the license to same-sex couples if the law permits them to marry. It makes no difference whether he thinks the law is just or wise. His role in satisfying the duty imposed upon him is similar to the decision-making process of an umpire.

For a judge, the obligation to obey the law, or, more accurately, apply the law in making decisions is very different from the role of the marriage-license clerk because a judge has the legal authority to make the law. The judge is subject to power-conferring secondary rules about how she makes the law. She takes an oath to apply the law, but she also has the authority to decide what the law is, and, in doing so, she may change the pre-existing law.[148] This sounds quite circular when you describe it in this way, but judges, acting as judges are supposed to act, and are authorized to act, have the authority to determine what the law is and to change the law in the process of doing so. There are self-executing customary norms governing how judges do so. I develop this concept of customary norms in much more detail in *The Judge and the Philosopher*.

My initial starting point in this book is to demonstrate why a judge is not like an umpire. I reject the premise that the judicial role is like calling balls and strikes. The thesis that a judge acts like an umpire reflects an effort to make judging appear mechanical, as though the judge merely applies pre-existing law to factual situations and the resultant decision is automatic.

Lower courts, however, must follow the rulings of higher courts in order to avoid being reversed if there is an appeal filed from one of their decisions. To avoid reversal, lower courts must anticipate how appellate courts will rule on an appeal. But, as Lawrence Baum, a political science professor at Ohio State University, points out, "the norm of obedience to higher courts is only one of many forces that shape judicial behavior, and it can be outweighed by other forces."[149] Lower courts even have to, in fact, anticipate, in the extreme case, the potential overruling of a precedent by the higher court.[150] The higher court may also reach a just decision or a wise decision. For a potential Supreme Court justice to claim that his role as a judge is like that of an umpire appears to be an effort to hide the human, moral, ethical and other factors involved in making judgments concerning human conduct.[151]

The law is, as Hart describes it, ascertained in accordance with the rule of recognition, which identifies the legal rules that form the pre-existing law. The correct decision is a judicial decision made by applying a legal rule of the pre-existing law in order to make the decision and this decision is presumptively justified. Every judicial decision should be justified either by applying a legal rule of the pre-existing law or by a reason that overrules making the correct decision.

Creative positivism recognizes justice and wisdom, as I have defined them, to be acceptable reasons for overriding the correct decision.

These reasons may be called extra-legal in the sense that they are not part of the pre-existing law (which makes them "extra"), but they are legal because they are permitted sources for judicial decision-making pursuant to Hart's other two secondary rules (besides the rule of recognition) the rule of adjudication and the rule of change. Moreover, the just decision and the wise decision are authorized, authoritative and binding decisions.

Correctness, justice and wisdom are the three elements of the judicial process. They may be viewed as three overlapping circles. A single decision could be in all 3 circles, or it could be in 2 or 1 of the circles. The three elements provide for, and make it possible for the law to be, both stable and changing at the same time.

The legal system includes, in addition to the legal rules, principles, policies, standards and values (collectively "policies"). Hart recognized that the law (putting aside the legal system) consists of only the rules, and creative positivism would agree with this approach. Creative positivism disagrees with Hart on what the law is, with some supplementation of Hart's description of the rule of recognition. But Hart believes that judges always apply the law unless they make a mistake, or they exercise discretion. Hart accepts that judges exercise discretion and make the law in hard cases when the law is indeterminate. I maintain that judges also make new legal rules in what Hart would consider to be easy cases (easy in those cases because the law is determinate). Hart maintains that judges do not have discretion to avoid applying the law in easy cases.

Creative positivism is a form of positivism because it recognizes the importance of the correct decision and acknowledges that judges generally try to and do make the correct decision. A creative positivist will differ from other positivists regarding how and when judges exercise discretion. Creative positivism accepts that the just decision and the wise decision may overrule the correct decision and that doing so will result in an authorized, authoritative and binding decision. The judge also has discretion in all cases to make the correct decision and to avoid or disregard evaluation of the legal rule being applied, and evaluation of the decision being made in applying the rule.

The focus of creative positivism is on the sources of judicial decisions. Adjudication consists of more than applying the pre-existing law. Courts are courts of justice in addition to being courts of law. They have the authority to make changes in the rules (law-making) and, for this task, the rule-makers look to policies, which includes principles.

John Gardner, another Professor of Jurisprudence at Oxford University, takes a slightly different approach:

> "Law is not the practice of producing legal norms (law-making). It is the practice of **using** legal norms (law-applying). Yet, its central and most distinctive creativity is a combination of the two: the production of legal norms by the use of legal norms (law-making by law-applying)."[152]

My problem with this approach is that it seems to imply that the legal rule that was used to decide the case was somehow in existence before it was applied, as though it was found and not created. This is true of self-executing customary norms that are applied for the first time in a judicial proceeding but not of other norms that are created out of whole cloth and do not exist before they are made. Gardner also is disregarding the conflict between the legal rule in the pre-existing law that is not being applied and the legal rule that is being created if the decision is not a correct decision.

While it is not true that the legal rules have always existed before they were applied in the decision, the element of plausibility in Gardner's view is that there are policies (or principles) inherent in the political, social and cultural systems that have influenced the legal system and ithe norms to be applied to make the judicial decision. These incorporated ideals are part of the legal system (though not part of the law) and the judge may look to them in making the just and/or the wise decision.[153]

A good example of the incorporation of principles into making a judicial decision would be the recent decision (September 24, 2019) by the Supreme Court of the United Kingdom regarding Prime Minister Johnson's prorogation of the Parliament.[154] Another example of a judicial decision involving the U.S. Constitution, the 12th Amendment to the Constitution, federal statutes, state statutes and self-executing constitutional customary norms is *Gohmert v. Pence* (January 2, 2021). In this case, a U.S. Congressman and a slate of nominee-electors (electors for Trump as opposed to electors for Biden who had won the election in Arizona which was being challenged in this case) filed a novel case to overturn the election result. The District Court, whose decision was affirmed by the Court of Appeals, held that the plaintiffs lacked standing to bring the case. This was the first time this specific type of challenge to the constitutionality of the electoral system for electing the president had been raised (which illustrates again that there are no gaps in the law, even in a case involving a claim that was unique in American jurisprudence).[155]

Creative positivism, as used in reference to judicial decision-making, seems on the surface to be contradictory. How can a judge apply pre-existing law and also be creative since creativity implies novelty and originality? It might be argued that judges must be mechanical (apply pre-existing law without exercising discretion) or creative, but not both at the same time. There is obviously creativity involved in constructing an alternate source decision, but creativity is also involved but less obviously so when the correct decision is made.

It might be suggested that the decision must be either correct (which is presumptively justified) or incorrect and therefore, unjustifiable. I maintain, however, that there are instances when the decision can be incorrect and still be a good (the best) decision and be an authorized decision, assuming that the decision will qualify as the just decision or the wise decision. I have provided examples of such decisions in this book. I will expand upon and explain in more detail these concepts in the books that will be published after this book.

This theory that I am proposing presupposes that judicial decisions will be justified by an application of a legal rule of the pre-existing law or by a reason that overrides the application of the pre-existing law based on consideration of relevant principles that would lead to a just and./or wise decision. These general principles are not part of the pre-existing law, but they are sources for acceptable and justifiable judicial decisions.

Consequently, applying the reasons that support just and wise decisions is ultimately legal (consistent with the norms of the legal system) because the judge's decision will be authorized, authoritative and binding. The converse is also true—the judge's decision will be authorized, authoritative and binding because it is legal. One should question whether the decisions of a judge who decides cases by flipping a coin would be authorized, authoritative and binding. This is an example of a self-executing customary rule of the legal system that upon appellate review, if this method for deciding cases was proven, would call for invalidating the decision made by flipping a coin.

Creative positivism differs from the theories of some of the American Legal Realists because they assert that any case could be decided for either party. Creative positivism, to the contrary, maintains that there is a correct decision in every case, though the court may consider whether that decision would be just and/or wise and may decide to reach an alternate source decision.

Hart resurrected the correct decision after some of the American Legal Realists had proclaimed that there was no such thing as a correct decision. He put judicial decision making in the framework of a legal system, described how and why legal systems become legitimate and, in doing so, gave legal positivism a prominent role in jurisprudence. Creative positivism differs from Hart's version of positivism because he contends that discretion is employed only in the hard cases (gaps in the law, open texture of the legal rules, or penumbral cases) and that there is no possible correct decision in those cases. I have accepted much of Hart's reasoning, but I have transformed his theory in order to provide for evaluation of judicial decisions.

Even if judges do not actually strive to reach correct, just or wise decisions, the decisions can be discussed in terms of whether they are correct, just or wise. The value that can be derived from discussing judicial decisions in these terms is that different aspects of the decisions can be distinguished, and, if this vocabulary is generally adopted, there would be clearer communication and understanding about judicial decisions.

My final task is to summarize why the role of a judge is not similar to the role of an umpire, which is the subject of the next chapter.

II.
CONCLUSION

11.1 Judges are not like umpires

There is a slight similarity between the role of a judge and the role of an umpire. They both operate pursuant to a system of rules that they apply to make judgments subject to customary norms as to the procedure for doing so. Applying rules to factual situations is a rational decision-making process. Decisions made by judges and umpires are either-or decisions and must be made (there are no gaps in the closed and comprehensive network of rules being applied). They both strive to reach correct decisions, though they may make mistakes. Even if mistakes are made, the decisions are final unless they are reversed by a higher authority. Finally, umpires and judges both sometimes make decisions as a group and other times as individuals.

The differences between judges and umpires are much more significant than the similarities. Therefore, the analogy is misleading and does not portray an accurate picture of judicial decision-making. Let's start with the differences in group decision-making. The umpires may confer with each other, and the decision will be made by the group or by the superior official within the group. The procedure within a panel of judges is markedly different. The judges may all agree, and one opinion will be written. Alternatively, as I discussed in Section 8.6, at the appellate level (and less frequently at the trial court level), judges act as a panel of judges. The judges who agree with the result but not with the reason for the decision may write a concurring opinion. Judges who disagree with the result may write a dissenting opinion.

The point I just made about panels of judges illustrates another very important difference between judges and umpires. Judges give reasons for their decisions; umpires do not have to give reasons. Judges write opinions defending their point of view; umpires do not do so. In other words, as I explained in Section 3.6, judges not only make rational decisions, but they make rational, reasoned decisions and they explain the reasons for their decisions.

Moreover, umpires must make decisions when the action occurs. Judges may take their time to reflect upon the decision and not make it for days, weeks, or months after the issue is presented to the court. This is not true of decisions made during the trial, such as rulings on evidence, but judges may pause in the trial and think about and research an evidentiary point before making the decision. Umpires cannot, in general, suspend the game and request the players to return the next day to resume the contest.

In addition, the appellate process in the judicial system is more established, institutionalized, systematic and is much more frequently invoked in judicial systems in comparison with the appeals process in sports. The doctrine of *stare decisis* (the legal principle of deciding cases according to rules established in precedents) imposes restraints upon lower-level judges and upon judges at the same level at which the precedent was made in that jurisdiction. Enforcing the following of precedents significantly affects judicial decision-making. Reversal aversion is common among lower-level judges. There is no procedure similar to this institutionalized established organized system of precedent-following and appellate reversal that applies to umpires.

The most important difference between judges and umpires is that the judge may create new rules and the umpire has no such authority.

Unlike umpires making decisions, judges making judicial decisions have the authority to make alternate source decisions. They may make, and they do make, just decisions and wise decisions. Sometimes, the just decision and/or the wise decision will not be the correct decision. Judges have the authority to make incorrect decisions (not incorrect because a mistake has been made) in order to make the best decisions. Umpires have no authority to deviate from the applicable rules to make just and/or wise decisions rather than correct decisions. Justice, morality and policymaking have no counterpart in the umpiring process.

Another importance difference between judges and umpires is that the legal rules are much more complex than the rules of baseball and the interpretation of legal rules is more systematized and organized than the interpretation of baseball rules. Interpretation of rules established in judicial decisions is reported in published decisions. The judge has more discretion than an umpire would have in interpreting the rules and has the ultimate authority, dependent somewhat on the level of the court, to overrule an interpretation of an existing rule or to modify the interpretation that was established in a prior case.

In addition to interpreting rules, judges may create new rules, or exceptions to rules, or contractions or extensions of rules. This is a creative process. It is beyond the scope of this book for me to go much further into legal reasoning, the procedure for extracting legal rules from precedents, deciding cases by analogy to other cases, eliminating potential conflicts in the rules, evaluating legal rules by considering legal principles, and other facets of the judicial process. I am leaving those subjects for *The Judge and the Philosopher*.

I do have one final point to make about the judicial process that differentiates judges from umpires. It is not unusual that a lawsuit will involve issues considerably more substantial and important than the outcome of a baseball game (including even the seventh game of the world series). In *Gohmert v. Pence*, the issue raised was an attack upon the validity of the election of Joseph B. Biden, Jr. to become the President of the United States.[156] The plaintiffs sought to have the electors pledged to former President Donald Trump recognized as the legal electors and the electors pledged to Joe Biden prohibited from having their votes counted. At stake was the 2020 election for President of the United States. Certainly, no umpire in any game had to make a decision with the consequences associated with this decision.

11.2 Supplementing Hart's *The Concept of Law*

Judges not only find, ascertain and recognize law, but they create new law that they apply rather than the law provided to them by Hart's rule of recognition. In other words, when the court acting pursuant to the rule of change creates a new legal rule, the law that is being applied is not the rule that would have been applied pursuant to the rule of recognition. Hart does not discuss the disregarding of the rule of recognition in order to make a new legal rule pursuant to the rule of change. Creative positivism accepts the legal theory that judges may make just and/or wise decisions that may be, but do not necessarily have to be correct decisions, and these decisions will be authorized, authoritative and binding.

Another type of law is the self-executing customary norm which is waiting to be recognized as law but is not enacted law before being recognized. While Hart accepts that customary norms may be law, he does not explain how this phenomenon affects the rule of recognition when the self-executing customary norm conflicts with the legal norm that would have been recognized pursuant to the rule of recognition. In short, in this instance, the law that is applied is different from the law that would be recognized if the self-executing customary norm was not applied.

A third major departure from the rule of recognition occurs when the real rules (rather than the paper rules, which are the enacted rules) are considered. These real rules, the law in action, cannot be ignored because they are the rules that affect human behavior. Their existence is a qualifying factor related to the general acceptance of the law by the law-subjects and the law-appliers. In other words, the rules being applied may not be the exact same rules that exist in the statute books or in the precedents.

In addition, Hart's description of the types of rules should be supplemented to include various situations in which the very nature of a "rule" is challenged. For example, President Biden issues an Executive Order declaring that Turkey committed genocide against the Armenians during and after World War I. Governor Tom Wolf of Pennsylvania requires that masks be worn because of the Covid pandemic but there is no penalty for not wearing a mask. Congress requires in the Affordable Care Act (Obamacare) that each adult individual must purchase medical insurance or pay a penally, and it reduces the penalty to $0 dollars. None of these examples fit easily into either Hart's duty-imposing rules or power-conferring rules. I will discuss these examples and many other similar situations in *The Judge and the President*.

While legal philosophy starts with the law, and the law consists of the primary rules and the secondary rules as Hart described the law, Hart's legal theory should be modified by accepting a third type of rules, which I call "tertiary rules." The law and the legal system are much more complex in a modern democratic society than Hart's legal theory would accommodate. Hart is trying to provide us with the skeleton that is common to all legal systems when the organs, bones and central nervous system are disregarded. But the skeleton does not provide an accurate picture of the way the law functions. I will describe the tertiary rules in *The Judge and the Incorrect Decision*.

Before I discuss these additional features of rules in a modern democratic legal system, I want to dig deeper into the existing legal theories and contrast those theories with creative positivism. Creative positivism is not intended to be a substitute for Hart's legal theory but is, instead, offered as a supplement to Hart's presentation of the primary and secondary rules. Consequently, in my next book, *The Judge and the Philosopher*, I will expand upon my description of Hart's legal theory, and I will discuss other legal theories in order to provide the foundation for creative positivism.

APPENDICES

APPENDIX A: Interview with Judge Thomas Gavin

I interviewed Judge Thomas Gavin on January 19, 2012, in his chambers in the Chester County Courthouse in West Chester, Pennsylvania. It was a 75-minute conference, and we covered a wide variety of topics. We talked about the *O'Brien v. Desco* case at some length. Here are some of the subjects we discussed.

Level of court: Judge Gavin was a trial-court judge. The reader will recall that Judge Gavin mentioned in the *O'Brien* case that the decision he made was not necessarily the moral or ethical decision. He told me that it was his view that the higher the level of court the greater the opportunity there is to incorporate your views of morality in making decisions.

Inadequate consideration—I asked him why he had not decided the case on the issue of inadequate consideration, which was the principal argument raised by O'Brien. He said that the payment of $500 to someone making six figures is not really enough money for them to give up their livelihood, but you have to consider when the payment was made. If the payment had been offered at the beginning of employment, when there was no history of income, the payment might have been adequate. Here, it was being offered when the employee had extensive knowledge. He knew the business when the payment was made to him. I asked Judge Gavin if he had avoided deciding the case on this issue in order to discourage an appeal. He said that he never thinks about encouraging or discouraging an appeal. It is not a factor for him. I asked him about reversal aversion. He said that is important to some judges but not to him. He gives it his best judgment and so be it.

If he were an appellate-court judge—I asked him if he would have approached the case differently if he were an appellate-court judge, and he said that he would. He explained the distinction between different levels of courts. At the trial level, he is primarily calling balls and strikes. For example, if there is a criminal case, and if he believes the defendant is guilty, but the prosecutor does not prove the case, he will find the defendant not guilty. He mentioned that sometimes he will state in his opinion that the law should be changed, and he sends the opinion to the legislature.

The decision in the *O'Brien* case—He said that the plaintiff (O'Brien) had started his own business. The defendant (Desco), which had an established business, had a clear and dramatic competitive advantage. That is why he thought that the non-compete agreement was not reasonably necessary to protect the defendant. If the employer has a good relationship with its customers, the employee cannot do too much damage. In addition, no trade secrets were involved. Judge Gavin said: "I can go into this rebar business tomorrow. It is not very complicated. The potential customers are obvious." Then, he said that the non-compete cases are very fact intensive. When the employee starts working, and he gets trained, and he signs a non-compete agreement at the inception of employment, he is not thinking about the effect of signing it, but that is a different situation. Then, he added that the non-compete agreements are disfavored by appellate courts. I asked him if it would make a difference if Desco had called its lawyer as a witness and the lawyer testified about the research, he had done in preparing the agreement. He said that it would make no difference. But he agreed that reliance can be a factor in some cases. He then gave the example of a higher-level employee being hired by a drug company. He said that the drug company required that the employee have a lawyer read the non-compete agreement which is a long document. The employee knows what he is doing when he signs it. The employee would know that it is serious, and Judge Gavin would enforce it. He then said that he looks to see if the restriction is reasonable in time and geography. For example, if it said 50 miles from Philadelphia, it would cover so much territory that it could be unreasonable. He repeated that these cases are fact intensive.

His moral views—He said that the perfect result in a case would be correct, moral and ethical, and that these are different standards. We discussed the Nazi situation from the Fuller/Hart debate, and he said that he would not enforce those immoral laws (the debate was about a case after the war had ended in which the wife had reported that her husband, during the wartime period, had violated the Nazi laws). He viewed the judges who applied the Nazi laws as having abused their power. I then mentioned the southern judges after the *Brown* decision, and he acknowledged that different people have different moral standards. He then offered an example. As a Catholic and as a human being, he believes that abortion is wrong. However, he has ordered that prisoners be released from prison in order to have an abortion. This issue, despite his personal view, has been resolved by the Supreme Court, and he enforces their precedents, even though he considers some of them to be immoral and unethical.

APPENDIX B: My experience as a law clerk for a trial judge

My experience as a law clerk for a trial-court judge when I was a young lawyer may illuminate some of the ideas that I am discussing. My duties included attending the trials, doing legal research and writing opinions, drafting charges to the jury and memoranda of legal issues. I noticed that the judge I served operated differently in jury trials than non-jury trials. In the jury trials, he made his rulings on the evidence, while trying not to let the jury know which way, he thought the jury should decide the case. He gave a fair charge, I believe, to the jury that was consistent with the pre-existing law (at least as consistent as I could make it since I wrote the charge for him) and he summarized the evidence fairly and accurately. He almost always accepted the verdict of the jury.

The procedure of the judge I clerked for in non-jury trials was completely different. I asked him one day at which point in the trial did he make his decision and he said that he did so in the first 30 minutes of the trial (though he added that it was possible that he might change his mind later in the trial). Obviously, he was very experienced, and he had excellent intuition. Also, before the trial, he would have read the pleadings, decided pre-trial motions, looked at all discovery documents that had been filed, he often knew the lawyers and he would have had an opportunity to observe the parties and witnesses who were talking to the parties. I almost always agreed with his judgment in the case.

During the non-jury trial, he would decide all motions in favor of the attorneys who represented the side that would be the ultimate loser. He would thank both attorneys for having tried a good case and the parties for having been truthful and honest. He would always, however, base his decision on the credibility of the witnesses. He explained to me that he employed these two procedures (deciding motions in favor of the losing party and basing the decision upon the credibility of the witnesses) in order to avoid being reversed by an appellate court (and he was very rarely reversed). Reversal aversion is very common in the trial courts.

The interesting point about this experience is that I thought that virtually all of this trial judge's decisions related to the ultimate outcome of the case would qualify as correct decisions. He had a strong intuitive sense of the law and he, as far as I could observe, never did legal research. His decisions were instinctive, and they were good decisions.

My primary goal in this book is to suggest a vocabulary for studying, analyzing, evaluating and criticizing judicial decisions. Evaluating judicial decisions is a process that is different from making judicial decisions. My approach, therefore, is conceptual in nature.

I would agree with the American Legal Realists that there are judges unlike the trial judge I clerked for who do not know the law, some who are impulsive, some who are irrational and a few who are not very intelligent. Most of the judges with whom I have had personal experience are serious, hardworking and competent. My focus has not been on individual judges but on individual cases that illustrate the points that I am making.

Since I have included examples from my own experience, (there are more of them in *The Judge and the Philosopher*) and I include within my legal philosophy attention to real rules and self-executing customary rules (in *The Judge and the President*), I cannot avoid describing the legal world as I see it. Therefore, the approach that I have taken could be viewed as somewhat descriptive.

Finally, if judges assume that their decisions will be evaluated, they may want to self-evaluate their decisions. To the extent that they do so, and assuming that the approach that I have taken is somewhat instructive, they could adopt a similar methodology to that presented in this book. In that limited sense, and if that happens, this book may be useful in how cases are decided. The author of a book can never know exactly what reaction, if any, his book will have.

APPENDIX C: Practical use of jurisprudential theories

I have practiced law in the United States for close to 50 years. I have tried many jury trials, many more non-jury and arbitration proceedings and appeared before many judges in pre-trial motions and other proceedings. I have also participated in hearings before various governmental agencies.

I have traveled to and represented clients in Australia, Canada, China, Hong Kong, Iceland, Isle of Man, Malaysia, Mexico, New Zealand, Puerto Rico, Singapore and Thailand. In addition, I have lived in and practiced law to a limited extent for two years in England and one year in Mexico.

In all these jurisdictions, I had to research and try to understand their historical and cultural backgrounds and how their legal systems functioned. The history and culture of individual nations around the world is unique to each locale. It is often very different from the culture and the legal systems in the United States and England, which are also different from each other (though the legal systems in Australia and Canada have some close similarities to those in the U.S. and England).

Hart tried to provide a framework for **all** legal systems, but satisfying that goal is very difficult. There are just too many variables in legal systems and legal cultures in the world. Let me provide one example.

I made several trips to China in the 1980's working on a project. My client wanted to lease 5,000 acres in Hainan Island in order to create an aloe vera farm and a large resort with hotels, restaurants, entertainment facilities and casinos. We negotiated a 99-year lease agreement of more than 100 pages. I attempted to think of every possible contingency and to cover how it would be resolved in the contract. My greatest difficulty was with the issue of how conflicts would be resolved.

Hainan Island is in the South China Sea, and it is one of many islands in that area. It was part of the Guangdong province, but the government on the island was actively seeking to be recognized as a separate province. It ultimately became part of a province consisting of multiple islands, and it was designated as a Special Economic Zone.

The first problem I had was to try to figure out which governmental entity—the local officials on the island, the officials of the province on the mainland, or those of the national government—had the ultimate authority to enter into the 99-year lease agreement. I never fully resolved that issue, and it seemed as though all three levels of government had some degree of control over the project, though the power of each level of government never became very clear.

The next issue was to find out what the laws were. China at that time had a socialist legal system. The legal system was generally based upon the civil law model (the system generally used in Europe based upon Roman law which I had studied at Oxford). While there was a detailed criminal code, there was no established civil code. In China, even though it has a long history of codes, the provisions in the codes did not generally regulate the enormous variety of commercial activities.

The hierarchy of the Chinese courts was confusing, and, ultimately, it made no difference because all the courts were subject to the authority of the Communist Party of China. If there was a dispute, it was not clear which judicial entity would have jurisdiction and whether the issue would be resolved by a judicial entity or a political entity.

None of the features of a legal system with which I was familiar existed in China at that time. There were no juries, no system of precedents and no independent judiciary. Judges in making decisions consulted with people's assessors and neighborhood committees of lay persons. Judges were poorly paid and regularly supplemented their salaries with gifts from litigants. China was just beginning to reform its legal system in order to establish a functioning institution.

While judges consulting neighborhood committees to make their decisions would appear odd to an Anglo-American lawyer, the influence of the neighborhood committees seemed similar to me to the importance of the opinions of the neighbors in zoning variance cases (this legal procedure is discussed in an Appendix about zoning law in one of the books that will be published after this book). I view both situations (the zoning variance in the U.S. and the neighborhood councils in China) as illustrative of real rules and self-executing customary rules (which I discuss in *The Judge and the President*).

The corruption of the judges in China was not very different from the corruption in the traffic court system in Philadelphia (this is also discussed in another book that will be published after this book) and the corruption in the judicial system in Mexico in the 1960's when I practiced law there. In fact, the influence of the political party, the Communist Party in China, was not that far removed from the influence of the urban political machines in the U.S. during much of the Twentieth Century.

There were appellate courts in China, but they did not function like the appellate courts with which I was familiar because they did not wait for appeals but could act on their own and they could make their own findings of fact. It was unclear where law-making authority ultimately rested, and there was no well-established system of legislation. The interpreter explained to me that there were no Chinese words that could be used to translate legal concepts from English to Chinese.

I came to understand that commercial disputes were rarely resolved in judicial proceedings. There were no established procedures for the filing of lawsuits or even for arbitration. After much discussion, which was long, tedious and strained, the contract we were working on included a provision for financial disputes to be resolved in Hong Kong (Hong Kong was still an English colony when this contract was being negotiated and it had a common-law legal system and a judicial system based on English law and traditions). All other disputes could be the subject of an arbitration in Switzerland. While these provisions were in the contractual document, the concepts were so foreign to the Chinese negotiators that I did not believe that they were really agreeing to these procedures.

This illustrates how difficult it is to draft contracts. I did not anticipate the changes that would occur in Hong Kong, though I knew the termination date on the agreement between the government in China and the United Kingdom. I did not expect the Chinese to assume complete control over Hong Kong and to dismantle much of the institutional structure set in place by the English.

This, then, leads to the broader question of whether the types of legal systems that we have been discussing in this book and this Appendix are fairly representative of the legal systems in civil law jurisdictions. Codes have existed for a long time in the civil law jurisdictions in Europe (Justinian Code, Napoleonic Code and various national codes, and China also had a long history of codes). Civil law systems do not generally recognize the concept of binding precedents. Rather, they rely on detailed codes that do not offer the same methods for interpretation that exist in common law jurisdictions. The codes are constantly updated, which eliminates some of the problem of ancient statutes.

The concept of judges as lawmakers is not the same in civil law countries as it is in the Anglo-American legal systems. In contrast to the common law jurisdictions, judge-made law in judicial decisions does not usually exist and the judicial decisions, in that sense, are not authoritative in civil law countries, though they are binding.

While there may be codes in specific fields of law in the common law countries, the legal systems in civil law countries are entirely codified. The codes, then, are the primary source of the law, and the text writers who explain and expand upon the code have a significant influence on its interpretation.

In a modern code, the values are often explicitly stated, and the principles derived from these values are frequently presented. The codes include principles within the law. The "primary rules" are in more general terms than the primary rules in a common law jurisdiction. While there is no established sense of precedents as being authoritative and binding, there may be an effort for consistency in interpretation of the provisions of the code being interpreted.

The judicial decisions may, however, not be reported in civil law jurisdictions, since the concept of a binding precedent does not exist. Law libraries, like the typical law library in an American law school, do not exist in the civil law countries. In the United States, however, the growing number of unpublished cases creates a situation that resembles the operation of the legal system in a civil law nation. I discuss unpublished decisions in the United States in the books that follow this book.

Moreover, in civil law jurisdictions, becoming a judge is a career decision, while judges are drawn from the pool of lawyers in common law countries. Judges take a more active role in questioning witnesses and finding the facts in civil law jurisdictions in comparison to common law jurisdictions. The system of grand juries in the U.S. is different from judges conducting investigations and acting as prosecutors in the civil law world.

Judges in the U.S. are products of the political system. The path to become a judge in the various states is different. In the federal system, judges are appointed and confirmed as part of a political process. In England, the judges are selected from the pool of barristers, who have trial experience. Many judges in the U.S. have had no trial experience, but they do generally have pollical connections. In many of the European civil law systems, the judges are civil servants who receive training for a career on the bench.

Just as common law jurisdictions may have codes in specific areas of the law, some jurisdictions have a blended civil law and common law system. Puerto Rico, for example, has a code that is heavily influenced by common law themes. Some countries, like Iceland, have a hybrid character, with a mix of civil law and Scandinavian customary law that is partially codified. Some nations incorporate religious law into their codes. This is typical of countries that recognize Islamic law

(I will discuss in a future book the possibility of Islamic law being a permissive source of law in Oklahoma based upon a case decided there, so there is some similarity in at least that jurisdiction).

Research of the law in the Anglo-American legal systems involves study of the law by reading the line of cases leading to the development of a legal rule that can then be utilized in the drafting of a contract. In the civil law world, the relevant legal rule is found within a comprehensive code that must be interpreted to find the applicable legal rule. While this is somewhat comparable to interpreting a statute, the degree of generality within the rules may be different.

While it is beyond the scope of this book to go into much more detail about civil-law jurisdictions, I should mention that the legal system in the State of Louisiana is partially a civil law legal system. The code in Louisiana is heavily influenced by the Napoleonic Code. Statutes and customs are sources of the legal norms that are in the code. Decisions of the U.S. Supreme Court are authoritative based upon the U.S. Constitution. There are trial courts, intermediate appellate courts and a Supreme Court in the state legal system. Decisions of higher courts are authoritative for inferior courts. So, there is a kind of *stare decisis* mechanism in judicial decision-making, but it is different than the common law systems in the other 49 states.

Federal courts applying Louisiana law in diversity cases follow the decisions of the Louisiana Supreme Court. If there is no decision that may be applied, the federal courts must guess what the law is (under the Erie Doctrine, legislation and custom are authoritative as they were pursuant to *Swift v. Tyson*).

Hart's theory of the open texture of the law bears some relevance to interpreting the provisions of a code. The idea of gaps, however, would appear to have no place in interpreting a code (and, as I have argued, really does not have any significance in common law jurisdictions). Similarly, the just decision and the wise decision do not seem to be relevant to a civil law jurisdiction in the same way that they are in common law jurisdictions. Both Hart's concept of law and creative positivism are strongly influenced by the common law traditions of judges interpreting statutes and precedents and engaging in law-making in deciding cases.

Based upon my experience, I doubt that Hart's concept of the legal system sounds the same to a civil law lawyer as it does to a common law lawyer. Some countries have had a tradition of codes going back thousands of years. In addition to the codes, just like the common law countries, the civil law countries also developed customary laws. In both types of legal systems, customary trade usages have an impact upon the interpretation of contracts. The origin of the common law is based upon customary rules and customary rules still play a significant role in common law countries and in civil law jurisdictions.

The traditions, mores and customs in the civil law countries are very different from those that are familiar to common law lawyers. My conclusion is that both Hart's concept of law and my theory of creative positivism are much more applicable to common law nations than they are to civil law states.

In the United States, in comparison to everywhere else in the world, there is a massive number of reported judicial decisions. Our law reporter system requires large libraries, with more books than you find in other jurisdictions. The number of precedents, and the corresponding amount of legal literature, developed in the U.S. in the 50 state jurisdictions with thousands of municipal court systems (including both trial courts and appellate courts in each state), and the federal judicial system, far exceeds those in any other nation.

In short, most of Anglo-American law has been developed in the process of adjudication, which is the source of the legal rules, developed when deciding individual cases. The bottom line is that Hart's focus on adjudication being the primary source, or one of the primary sources, of the legal rules does not accurately depict the civil law world. Legal rules there are not created by courts to the same extent as they are in common law jurisdictions.

Keeping in mind these vast differences, I still found that I approached each jurisdiction using the same legal-reasoning methodology that I had learned in an American law school and further developed at Oxford. Law was still law as I traveled to other countries and the legal system had some familiar attributes in those countries, though the Chinese legal system was difficult to qualify as a legal system. Every jurisdiction that has a legal system has a formula for finding the law (for distinguishing law from non-law) and the law exists as the law only if there is a legal system. In other words, I had some background for the discussions with the local lawyers in many different jurisdictions, and much of the vocabulary (the legal terminology that we used) was familiar (the lawyers usually spoke English, including the lawyers in the law firm that I was using for the contract in China which was a Hong Kong law firm).

A legally binding contract was a legally binding contract in every jurisdiction. Breach of contract was a familiar concept everywhere. Relief for the breach, both in terms of the procedure available and the method for computing damages, and even more so the systems for collecting the damages, were very variable, sometimes even questionable.

I found that I tended to conceptualize and compartmentalize based upon my Anglo-American background, education and training. I thought in terms of the primary and secondary rules, and I looked for analogies that were familiar to and related to the examples with which I was familiar.

My experience in practicing law in other countries reflects the accuracy of the observation of Peter J. Hamilton:

"Law is the expression of the rules by which civilization governs itself, and it must be that in law as elsewhere will be found the fundamental differences of peoples. Here then it may be that we find the underlying causes of the difference between the civil law and the common law."[157]

So, notwithstanding the enormous degree of difference, and the lack of familiarity initially with local customs and the initial strangeness of cultural differences, and always with the help of local lawyers, I managed to end up with legal contracts. The bottom line is that I felt like I was practicing law in many different countries and that the law is the law everywhere.

Notes

Chapter One: Judges Are Not Umpires

[1] Senatorial Confirmation Hearing on the Nomination of John G. Roberts, Jr. to be Chief Justice of the United States, *Hearings before the Senate Committee on the Judiciary*, 109th Congress, Page 55 (2005). See Harris, Richard, *Decision,* for a discussion of the nominating process for Supreme Court justices which is that the President has the power to nominate judges, and, with the advice and consent of the Senate, to appoint judges (Article II, Section 2 of the U.S. Constitution). Harris' book is about the nomination of G. Harold Carswell. The Senate did not approve the nomination when Senator Hruska, one of his supporters, commented that Carswell was only mediocre, but argued for his appointment so that all the mediocre people would have representation on the Supreme Court (Page 110).

[2] Senatorial Confirmation Hearing for Brett M. Kavanaugh, "Full Speech Brett Kavanaugh's opening statement at Senate Hearing," YouTube. http://www.youtube.com/watch?v=eahnOcp883k

[3] Kavanaugh, Brett M., "The Judge as Umpire: Ten Principles," YouTube, published April 1, 2015.
http://www.youtube.com/watch?v=SXKX_whwVzs. The speech also appears in an article format with the same title in 65 Catholic University Law Review 683 (June 22, 2015).

[4] Roberts exact words are: "I will decide every case based on the record, according to the rule of law, without fear or favor, to the best of my ability, and I will remember that it's my job to call balls or strikes, and not to pitch or bat." Roberts, John, supra note 1 at 56.

[5] For further information about the relationship of language and decision making, see Ayer, A.J., *Language, Truth & Logic* and Pitkin, Hanna Fenichel, *Wittgenstein and Justice*.

[6] See Weber, Bruce, "Umpires v. Judges," *The New York Times,* July 11, 2009:

https://www.nytimes.com/2009/07/12/weekinreview/12weber.html

Weber refers to an example of an umpire being reversed by the Commissioner of Baseball, but this is a rare occurrence (the example occurs in a World Series game when the Commissioner was at the game). A modern judicial system has an established procedure for review of judicial decisions.

[7] Berman, Mitchell N., "'Let 'em play:' A study in the jurisprudence of sport," 99 Georgetown Law Journal 1325 (2011). Berman explains: " . . . [B]alls and strikes are not proper candidates for temporal variance because (1) temporal variance depends upon the widening of a gap between the competitive cost of an infraction and the competitive cost of the penalty it incurs, but (2) there is no such gap between nonconformity with a power-conferring rule and the consequences that attach, and (3) the rules governing balls and strikes are power-conferring rules (or something of a sufficiently close type)." Id. at 135. I will discuss power-conferring rules in Chapter Three.

[8] Official Rules of Baseball

http://mlb.mlb.com/documents/0/8/0/268272080/2018_Official_Baseball_Rules.pdf

[9] Weber, who is mentioned in EN6, points out that Justice Roberts had some difficulty defending the Supreme Court's decision in Brown v. Board of Education because that decision overruled the leading well-established precedent of Plessy v. Ferguson that had established the doctrine of "separate but equal." See *Brown v. Board of Education of Topeka*, 347 U.S. 483 (1954); *Plessy v. Ferguson*, 163 U.S. 537 (1896). Justice Roberts insisted that this did not amount to changing the strike zone. Roberts could have

said, if he followed the reasoning in this book, that the Brown decision was an alternate source decision (a wise decision) because it reflected the overriding public policy that segregation of schools is inconsistent with prevailing public policy and generally accepted constitutional principles. Weber refers to an umpire telling him that "It's [the strike zone] is like the Constitution. The strike zone is a living, breathing document."

The theory that judges decide all cases in accordance with pre-existing law was the predominant legal theory in the first half of the twentieth century. I call it the traditional theory, and I discuss it in greater length than in this book in *The Judge and the Philosopher.* This theory attempts to establish that the personal inclinations of the decision-maker is never a factor in making their decisions, which decisions are mechanical and do not involve judgment calls. This theory is not accepted by many legal philosophers and judges.

Judge Theodore McKee, also a Court of Appeals judge, contends that the comparison with umpires hides the effect of personal bias. He argues that the law is flexible and strong enough to allow for judge to be more honest about their approach. McKee, Theodore A., "Judges as Umpires," 35 Hofstra Law Review 1709, 1710-11 (2007).

Judge McKee then proposes the following: "Rather than indulging the pretense that judges are umpires and that umpires merely 'call them as they see 'um,' we should accept the fact that the law is flexible enough and strong enough to accommodate a fair more honest approach to adjudication**.**" Id. at 1719.

Judge Richard A. Posner presents the following analogy: "So against Chief Justice Roberts' umpire analogy, I see the story of the three judges asked to explain the epistemology of balls and strikes. The first umpire explains that he calls them as they are, the second that he calls them as he sees them, and the third that there are no balls and strikes until he calls them. The law professor is the first umpire. The modest formalist judge, who has no illusions that his method yield demonstrable truth, is the second umpire. The judge deciding cases in the open area is the third umpire; his activity is creative rather than discovery." Posner, Richard A., "The Role of the Judge in the Twenty-first Century," 86 Boston University Law Review 1049, 1051 (2006).

[10] Dworkin, Ronald, *The Supreme Court Phalanx*, Page 21: "Since Bork, all nominees claim to decide according to the rule of law and enforce the Constitution as it is rather than refer to their own personal bias." For further information about Senatorial confirmation hearings for Supreme Court nominees, see the following: Liptak, Adam, "Path to Supreme Court: Speak Capably, Say Little," *Politics*, July 11, 2009. https://www.nytimes.com/2009/07/12/us/politics/12judge.html

[11] See "Kavanaugh's 'judge as umpire' metaphor sounds neutral but it's deeply conservative," in "Why the Kavanaugh hearings were a show trial gone bad," *The Conversation*, October 7, 2018: http://theconversation.com/why-the-kavanaugh-hearings-were-a-show-trial-gone-bad-102025.

[12] See Weldon, P.D., *Vocabulary of Politics*, Page 67; Guest, A.G., "Logic and Law," *Oxford Essays in Jurisprudence,* Page 191; Ross, Alf, *On Law and Justice*, Page 11; Hart, H.L.A., "Scandinavian Realism," 1959 Cambridge Law Journal 233, 236; Hart, H.L.A., *The Concept of Law*, Pages 136-41; Kantorowicz, Hermann, *The Definition of Law,* Pages 89-90; Hart, H.L.A., *Definition and Theory in Jurisprudence, Essays in Jurisprudence and Philosophy*, Page 9 (first published in 1953). See also Llewellyn, Karl, *The Bramble Bush,* Pages 20-21.

[13] Ross, Alf, *On Law and Justice,* Page 11. For a description of the Scandinavian Legal Realists, see Green, Michael Stephen, "Legal Realism as Theory of Law," 46 William & Mary Law Review 1915, 1998-99 (2005).

[14] Hart, H.L.A., "Scandinavian Realism," 1959 Cambridge Law Journal 233, 239. See, however, Hart, H.L.A., *The Concept of Law*, Pages 136-37.

[15] Auerbach, Carl A., "On Professor Hart's Definition," 9 Journal of Legal Education 39, 46 (1956). For Hart's views on the definition of law, *see* Hart, H.L.A., "Definition and Theory in Jurisprudence." *Essays in Jurisprudence and Philosophy*, Page 21. (First published in 1953).

[16] "There are further rules laying down the proceedings at games, sports, entertainments and festivities, rules which are the soul and substance of the amusement or pursuit and are kept because it is felt and recognized that any failure to 'play the game' spoils it— that is, when the game is really a game. . . It is quite easy to follow the rule as not, and once you embark upon a sporting or pleasurable pursuit, you really can enjoy it only if you obey all the rules, whether of art, manners or the game." Malinowski, Bronislaw, *Crime and Custom in Savage Society*, Page 5.

[17] See Patterson, Edwin, *Jurisprudence*, Page 210.

[18] To be fair to Justice Kavanaugh, I should mention that he does sometimes qualify his assertion that judges operate like umpires. He notes that the judicial process is not mechanical decision making (this is his tenth principle). He also states that making decisions may require reasonable decision making. Finally, he acknowledges that deciding cases is not always pure interpretation. Kavanaugh, Brett M., "The Judge as Umpire: Ten Principles," supra, EN 3.

Chapter Two: The Correct Decision

[19] As stated in the text, every legal system has criteria for distinguishing non-binding promises from legally binding promises. In Roman law, there is no concept of consideration. In the Middle Ages, placing a seal on a document would result in a promise in the document being viewed as legally binding, but there was not an easy method for enforcement. In common law countries, the

courts developed the concept of consideration as being necessary for a promise or a contract to be legally binding.

Consideration may be either a detriment assumed by the promising party or a benefit to be received by the other party. Anything of value may constitute consideration. It need not be of equal value. It is the bargained-for benefit between the parties.

A similar concept is *quid pro quo* (Latin for "something for something"), which is a favor or advantage granted or expected in return for something. It was made famous by President Donald Trump's contention in 2019 that he had not offered Ukraine anything for investigating Joe Biden, his potential political opponent, when he was withholding military aid provided by Congress. This request was the primary focus of Trump's first impeachment trial.

For a discussion about consideration see Holmes, Oliver Wendell, Jr., *The Common Law*, Page 273. See also Hunter, William A., *Introduction to Roman* Law, Page 92 and Buckland, W.W. and McNair, Arnold D., *Roman Law and Common* Law, Pages 221-37. Consideration is discussed in more detail in Section 5.2. See also EN46.

[20] *O'Brien v. Desco Steel Corp.*, 57 Chester County Law Reporter 93 (2009). The facts of the case, which I have summarized, are presented in Judge Gavin's opinion.

[21] Id. at 97. In Appendix B, I discuss my experiences as a law clerk for a trial judge. The judge I clerked for always mentioned in his opinions that he found the witnesses to be more credible for the party that would prevail in the case. He did so because the likelihood of a reversal on an appeal is diminished if the decision of the trial judge is based upon the credibility of the witnesses. The appellate court does not see or hear the witnesses and gets a typed transcript of their testimony. Judge Gavin did not follow a similar practice and he held that the party that lost the case, the witness for Desco, was the credible party and that the party that won the case lacked credibility. In Appendix A, I include my notes

from an interview of Judge Gavin, and he stated that the possibility of reversal on an appeal does not factor into his decision-making and that his fact-finding in the O'Brien case would be consistent with that statement.

[22] Ibid.

[23] Ibid.

[24] Ibid.

[25] Id. at 98.

[26] Id. at 97.

[27] Green, Leslie, Introduction to the Third Edition of Hart's *The Concept of Law,* Page xv.

[28] See Green, Michael Steven, "Legal Realism as Theory of Law," 46 William & Mary Law Review 1915, 1932 (2005). Consider the following: "Where Oliphant [who is one of the American Legal Realists] argues, for example, that the promise-not-to-compete cases are decided not by reference to law but by reference to uncodified norms prevalent in the commercial culture in which the disputes arose, this only shows that the law is indeterminate on the assumption that the normative reasons the courts are actually relying upon are not themselves legal reasons." I contend in *The Judge and the* Rules that self-executing customary norms are, in some instances, legal norms and, therefore, legal reasons for the correct decision. This quotation is from Leiter, Brian, "Legal Realism and Legal Positivism Reconsidered," 111 Ethics 278, 292 (2001): https://papers.ssrn.com/sol3/papers.cfm?abstract_id=761007/.

Chapter Three: Finding the Correct Decision

[29] Brian Bix refers to "legally determined outcomes" rather than the correct decision. Bix, Brian, "New Legal Realism and the Explanation for Judicial Behavior: Doctrine, Data and High Theory," SSRN 2519 606, Page 13:

https://papers.ssrn.com/sol3/papers.cfm?abstract_id=2519606.
See also Bix, Brian, "H.L.A. Hart and the Hermeneutic Turn in Legal Theory," 52 Southern Methodist University Law Review 167 (1999).

[30] I have borrowed this analogy from Joseph Raz, *Between Authority and Interpretation*. He uses this analogy to distinguish between change and loss of identity. The constitution, even though potentially changed by interpretation by the court, is still the same constitution. Similarly, the house you bought 20 years ago is the same house you now live in, although it has changed over the years. I have expanded upon the analogy.

[31] See Posner, Richard A., *Frontiers of Legal Theory*, Page 288.

[32] As mentioned in EN29, Brian Bix refers to "legally determined outcomes" rather than the correct decision. Bix, Brian, "New Legal Realism and the Explanation for Judicial Behavior: Doctrine, Data and High Theory," SSRN 2519 606, Page 13:
https://papers.ssrn.com/sol3/papers.cfm?abstract_id=2519606.
See also Bix, Brian, "H.L.A. Hart and the Hermeneutic Turn in Legal Theory," 52 Southern Methodist University Law Review 167 (1999).

[33] The court may find that the plaintiff failed to state a cause of action or did not satisfy the burden of proof. See, for example, *Thomas v. The Philadelphia Housing Authority*, 875 F.Supp. 272 (E.D. Pa.1995) in which the District Court found that the plaintiff failed to meet the required burden of proof. *See also Mohamad v. Palestinian Authority*, 566 U.S. 449 (2012), in which the Supreme Court found that the plaintiff did not state a cause of action when a Palestinian was killed by PLO intelligence officers because the Torture Victim Protection Act authorized civil lawsuits only against individuals who actually carried out the torture or accidental killing and not against the organization with which they were associated:
https://scholar.google.com/scholar_case?case=11200365666536967721&hl=en&as_sdt=6&as_vis=1&oi=scholarr.

Finally, *Conway v. Cutler Group, Inc.*, 25 Pa. D. & C.5th 239 (2012), which is discussed in Chapter Seven is a case which was decided on the basis that the plaintiff failed to state a cause of action. Sometimes, the basis for a decision declining jurisdiction is that the case is deemed to be non-justiciable which I discuss in *The Judge and the Rules.*

[34] Christie, George C., "The Universal Audience and Predictive Theories of Law," 5 Law and Philosophy, 343 (1986).

[35] Judge Richard A. Posner points out that judges do not differentiate between applying and making law. They do not declare: "Now, I will legislate." Posner, Richard A., *The Problematics of Moral and Legal Theory.* Thomas Schultz indicates that the officials operating within the legal system decide what they recognize as law, and thereby exercise the powers bestowed upon them by the system's legal rules. The official applies the law, as the official determines what is the law. Schultz, Thomas, "Why being law matters," *Transnational Legality: Stateless Law and International Arbitration,* Page 12. I contend, to the contrary, that it is important to distinguish between applying a rule of the pre-existing law and creating a new rule in order to determine whether the decision is correct or incorrect and that this determination is critical to analysis and criticism of judicial decisions.

Chapter Four: The Incorrect Decision

[36] PCBs are polychlorinated biphenyls.

[37] United States Constitution, Article III, Section Two.

[38] *Cincinnati Insurance Co. v. Flanders Motor Service Inc.,* 40 F.2d 146 (7th Cir. 1994).

[39] *Id.* at 150.

[40] *American States Insurance Co. v. Kiger*, 662 N.E.2d 945 (Ind. 1996). This was an action brought against a gas station in an effort

to recover gasoline contamination clean-up costs. The trial court found in favor of the insured. The Indiana Supreme Court affirmed. It held that "sudden and accidental" when used as an exception to pollution cleanup cost coverage was ambiguous about whether the meaning of "sudden" included a temporal element. Because it was ambiguous, the Supreme Court of Indiana concluded that it should be interpreted in favor of insurance coverage.

The insurance company argued that the clause should be interpreted as limiting coverage to those harms that occurred both abruptly and unintentionally. The insured argued for an interpretation that would provide coverage if the pollution was unexpected and unintended.

The exclusion reads as follows: "Bodily injury or property damage caused by the dumping, discharge or escape of irritants, pollutants or contaminants. This exclusion does not apply if the discharge is sudden and accidental." This provision was first added to insurance policies in the early 1970's.

Since a gas station was involved in this case, and since leakage of gasoline and motor oil is not uncommon in gas stations, it is not surprising that the Indiana Supreme Court found that there was insurance coverage. The insurance company had to be aware of the likelihood of pollution and could have drafted clearer language in its insurance policies.

Moreover, since the trial court found for the insured, the Court of Appeals in Cincinnati 1 should have anticipated that there was a real possibility that the decision of the trial court in Indiana would be affirmed by the Indiana Supreme Court.

[41] *Seymour Manufacturing Co., Inc. v. Commercial Union Insurance*, 665 N.E.2d 891 (Ind. 1990).

[42] *Cincinnati Insurance Co. v. Flanders Motor Service, Inc.*, 131 F. 3d 625, 39 Fed. R. SERV. 3d 454, 28 ENVTL L. Rep. 20, 339 (7th Cir. 1997).

[43] The Court of Appeals could have, if it concluded that Indiana law was unclear, certified the case to the Indiana Supreme Court for decision. *See Fross v. County of Allegheny*, 20 A.3d 1193 (Pa. 2011) where the case was referred to the Supreme Court of Pennsylvania by the Third Circuit Court of Appeals (the federal intermediate appellate court). The case concerned interpretation of Megan's Law, which requires individuals convicted of kidnapping, indecent assault or promoting of prostitution to register with local police for their residence for 10 years following release on probation or from prison.

[44] *Cincinnati Insurance Co. v. Flanders Motor Service, Inc.*, 131 F.3d at 629. Ernest A. Young raises the question of whether the federal court could decide that, if the state court did not decide the case the way the federal court thinks it should decide it, the state court could have made an incorrect decision. He argues that "it remains intelligible . . . to insist that a state court is 'wrong' about the content of state law, even state common law." But he concludes that "having been delegated authority to make law, it would not be possible for the state supreme court to be 'wrong' about the content of state law, and federal courts should defer accordingly." Young, Ernest A., "A General Defense of Erie Railroad Co. v. Tompkins," 10 Journal of Law, Economics and Policy 17 (2013). The Court of Appeals in Cincinnati 2 could apply federal law rather than state law because the Erie Doctrine only requires that the substantive law of the state be applied in diversity cases, so the Court of Appeals could apply federal procedural law and the finality-of-decision doctrine could be viewed as federal procedural law.

Chapter Five: The Just Decision

[45] *Webb v. McGowin*, 27 Ala.App. 82, 168 So. 196 (1935), <u>cert. denied,</u> 232 Ala. 374, 168 So. 199 (1936). <u>https://www.lexisnexis.com/community/casebrief/p/casebrief-webb-v-mcgowin-1152821028</u>.

[46] In an interesting lecture, *Webb v. McGowin* is compared to *Mills v. Wyman*, 20 Mass. 207 (1825). The court held in the *Mills* case that past consideration is no consideration. This is a case in which Mills cared for Wyman's emancipated son, who promised Mills that he would be paid for doing so. The court found for Mills and did not enforce the promise. It applied the general rule that a valid contract requires an offer, acceptance of the offer and consideration. See YouTube, "Contract Law 18 Mills v. Wyman and Webb v. McGowin (moral obligation)," Yale Courses filed on July 21, 2017: <u>https://www.youtube.com/watch?v=1KUMlqKtDhk</u>.
The Restatement of Contracts Section 86 Comments accept the decision in Mills v. Wyman as, what I am calling, the correct decision: "A gives emergency care to B's adult son while the son is sick and without funds far from home. B subsequently promises to reimburse A for his expenses. The promise is not binding under this Section." *Mills v. Wyman*, 20 Mass. 207 (Mass. 1825). See also:<u>https://www.casebriefs.com/blog/law/contracts/contracts-keyed-to-knapp/enforcing-promises-bases-of-legal-obligation/mills-v-wyman/</u>.
For the history of the law of contract, see Berman, Harold J., et al, *The Nature and Functions of Law*, Pages 529-677. Every legal system has a procedure for facilitating voluntary arrangements, such as legal norms for contracts to be binding. See also Shepherd, Harold and Sher, Bryan D., *Law in Society: An Introduction to Freedom of Contract*, Page 142. Consideration for contracts is discussed in EN19 and Section 5.2.

[47] *Lloyd v. Grace, Smith & Co.*, [1912] A.C. 716, 738.

[48] *Wilder Grain Co. v. Felker*, 296 Mass. 177, 179, 5 N.E.2d 207, 208 (Mass. 1936).

[49] *Id.* at 180 and 208. For a similar case, see *Todd v. Martin*, 37 P. 872 (Cal. 1894).

[50] *Hutson v. Hutson*, 168 Md. 182, 177 A. 177 (Md. 1935).

[51] *Liebman v. Rosenthal*, 185 Misc. 837, 57 N.Y.S. 875 (N.Y. Sup. Ct. 1945). One of the most famous decisions made by Lord Macnaghten, the judge in *Lloyd v. Grace, Smith & Co.*, the first case mentioned in this section, involved this same issue of parties *in pari delicto*. The case is *Gluckstein v. Barnes* [1900] AC 240. In this case, the fraudulent company promoters were denied relief when they sued other participants in the fraudulent activities. He ruled that the plaintiff had to look to the principle of honor among thieves in order to recover.

[52] Frank, Jerome N., "What Courts Do in Fact," 26 Illinois Law Review 645, 655 (1932).

[53] Frank, Jerome N., *Law and the Modern Mind,* Page 157.

[54] Frank, Jerome N., "Memorable Victories in the Fight for Justice," *Life Magazine*, Volume 30, March 12, 1951, Page 104.

[55] "In our society, the judges have developed the art of equity which controls fairness, tolerance, mercy, the spirit of kindliness. They seemingly adjust most rules to particular cases..."

"Here is the practice, the devotion, which comes from the very heart of democratic justice: reverence for the man—not the abstraction in capital letters but the man, the individual, seeking a good life. Here perhaps we come closest to the deep meaning of that majestic word, justice." Frank, Jerome N., "Memorable Victories in the Fight for Justice," *Life Magazine*, Volume 30, March 12, 1951, Page 102. See also Karl Llewellyn's poem, "Ballade of a Fungible Man," *Put in His Thumb*, Page 41.

[56] *Aero Spark Plug Co. v. B.G. Corp.*, 130 F.2d 290, 294, 298, n. 26 (2d. Cir. 1942) (Frank, J. concurring). J. Mitchell Rosenberg asserts that Frank preferred the just decision to the wise decision. Frank

also believes that the quest for certainty should never be subordinated to the quest for justice. Acting as a judge, however, Frank accepted established precedents in civil cases, even though he disagreed with them, while dissenting in criminal cases. Rosenberg, J. Mitchell, *Jerome Frank: Jurist and Philosopher*, Pages 69, 71, 79. To the contrary, Robert Jerome Glennon states that "[Frank] refused both to allow legal rules to stand in the way of just results and to pretend that two parties have entered fairly into a contract when in reality one side dictated the contractual terms." Glennon, Robert Jerome, *The Iconoclast as Reformer,* Page 138. For cases in which Judge Frank makes reference to his attempt to reach just decisions, see *Guiseppi v. Walling*, 144 F.2d 608, 618-19 (2nd Cir. 1944); and Ricketts v. Pennsylvania Railroad Co., 153 F.2d 757, 760 (2nd Cir. 1946) (Frank, J. concurring).

[57] Frank, Jerome N., *Courts on Trial,* Pages 266-70.

[58] Frank, Jerome N., *Courts on Trial,* Page 132. See also Frank, Jerome N., *Law and the Modern Mind,* Page 154.

[59] Frank, Jerome N., *Courts on Trial,* Pages 286-88.

[60] *Gavin v. Hudson Manhattan Railroad Co.*, 185 F.2d 104, 106 (3d. Cir. 1950). See also Corbin, Arthur Linton, "The Restatement of the Conflict of Laws," 15 Iowa Law Review 19, 35 (1929); Lorenzen, Ernest, "Territoriality, Public Policy and the Conflict of Laws," 33 Yale Law Journal 736, 750 (1924); and Radin, Max, "The Trail of the Calf," 32 Cornell Law Review 137, 145 (1946).

[61] Allen, Sir Carleton Kemp, *Aspects of Justice*, Page 56, n.1.

[62] Stammler, Rudolf, *The Theory of Justice* (translated by Isaac Husik), Page 94.

[63] Pound, Roscoe, *An Introduction to the Philosophy of Law*, Page 60.

[64] Id. at 52.

[65] Pound, Roscoe, "The Scope and Purpose of Sociological Jurisprudence," 24 Harvard Law Review 59 (Part 1, 1911), 25 Harvard Law Review 140 (Part 2, 1912), 25 Harvard Law Review 489, 515 (Part 3, 1912).

[66] *Pennsylvania Railroad Co.* at 760 (Frank, J. concurring), and *Repouille v. United States*, 165 F.2d 152, 154 (2d Cir. 1947) (Frank, J. dissenting).

[67] Rosenberg, J. Mitchell, *Jerome Frank: Jurist and Philosopher*, Page 63. Glennon stated that "Although his [Frank's] jurisprudential writings depicted judges as having unfettered discretion, his judicial position demanded that he abide by the customary rules of policy." Glennon, Robert Jerome, *The Iconoclast as Reformer*, Page 109.

[68] Rosenberg, J. Mitchell, *Jerome Frank: Jurist and Philosopher*, Page 63. Richard A. Posner observed that most judges are unmoved by the equities of the individual case, as most legal realists, other than Frank, realized. Posner, Richard A., *How Judges Think*, Page 119.

[69] Glennon, Robert Jerome, *The Iconoclast as Reformer: Jerome Frank's Impact on American Law*, Page 179.

[70] Rosenberg, J. Mitchell, *Jerome Frank: Jurist and Philosopher*, Page 53. Rosenberg asserted that Frank did not think that continuity outweighed justice, Id. at 53-54, though Frank's views on *stare decisis* definitely changed and he came to believe that a high percentage of cases could be disposed of by the routine application of the legal rules. Id. at 64.

[71] Glennon, Robert Jerome, *Frank: The Iconoclast as Reformer*, Page 151. Rosenberg insists that Frank, as a judge, was a little more ready than other judges to overrule precedents. Rosenberg, J. Mitchell, *Jerome Frank: Jurist and Philosopher*, Page 160.

[72] See Rosenberg, J. Mitchell, *Jerome Frank: Jurist and Philosopher*, Page 67, and Glennon, Robert Jerome, *The Iconoclast as Reformer,* Pages 105-09.

[73] Allen, Sir Carleton Kemp, *Law in the Making,* Page 283. See also Paton, George Whitecross, *Jurisprudence*, Page 153, n. 12; Cohen, M. R., *A Preface to Logic*, Page 73; and Wasserstrom, Richard, *The Judicial Decision*, Page 84.

[74] Pound, Roscoe, *Justice According to Law,* Pages 7-8.

[75] *Burnet v. Coronado Oil & Gas Co.*, 285 U.S. 393, 405-06, 52 S. Ct. 443, 446-47 (1932) (Stone, J. dissenting).

Chapter Six: The Wise Decision

[76] United States Constitution, Article III, Section 2

[77] The law that will be applied in the typical diversity-of-citizenship automobile accident case will be that of the state where the accident occurred, and it could also be the law of a foreign jurisdiction. See Walton v. Arabian American Oil Co., 233 F.2d 541 (2d Cir. 1956) (law of Saudi Arabia applied when the accident occurred there).

[78] Hurst, James Willard, *The Growth of American Law: The Law Makers*.

[79] Judiciary Act of 1789, Ch. 20, 34th Section. Section 34 is now codified at 28 U.S.C. Section 1652. For the history of the Judiciary Act, see Hurst, James Willard, *The Growth of American Law: The Law Makers*, Page 109.

[80] Ibid.

[81] *Swift v. Tyson*, 41 U.S. 1, 16 Pet. 1, 10 LEd. 865 (1842).

[82] *Bay v. Coddington*, 5 Johns Chan. Rep. 54 (1821).

[83] *Brush v. Scribner*, 11 Conn. Rep. 388 (1836).

[84] The Court of Common Pleas in Chester County in *O'Brien v. Desco Steel Corp.*, discussed in Chapter Two, may have been similarly motivated because Judge Gavin mentioned that the economic conditions were a factor, and he may have wanted to ensure that there was competition in the sale of steel rebars.

[85] *Erie Railroad Co. v. Tompkins*, 304 U.S. 64 (1938).

[86] *Black & White Taxicab & Transfer Co. v. Brown & Yellow Taxicab & Transfer Co.*, 276 U.S. 518, (1928).

[87] *Id.* at 528.

[88] *Black & White Taxicab & Transfer Co. v. Brown & Yellow Taxicab & Transfer Co.*, 276 U.S. 518 (1928) (Holmes, J. dissent).

[89] Ibid.

[90] *Tompkins v. Erie R. Co.*, 90 F.2d 603 (2d Cir. 1937).

[91] Justice Holmes had pointed out the difficulties presented by *Swift v. Tyson* in his dissenting opinion: "Law is a word used with different meanings, but law in the sense in which courts speak of it today does not exist without some definite authority behind it. The common law so far as it is enforced in a State, whether called common law or not, is not the common law generally but the law of that State existing by the authority of that State without regard to what it may have been in England or anywhere else. It may be adopted by statute in place of another system previously in force [case citation]. But a general adoption of it does not prevent the State Courts from refusing to follow the English decisions upon a matter where the local conditions are different {case citation]. It may be changed by statute {case citation], as is done every day. It may be departed from deliberately by judicial decisions, as with regard to water rights, in States where the common law generally prevails. Louisiana is a living proof that it need not be adopted at all. ...Whether and how far and in what sense a rule shall be adopted whether called common law or Kentucky law is for the State alone to decide.

"If within the limits of the Constitution a State should declare one of the disputed rules of general law by statute there would be no doubt of the duty of all courts to bow, whatever their private opinions might be. [case citation]. I see no reason why it should have less effect when it speaks by its other voice. [case citation]. If a State Constitution should declare that on all matters of general law the decisions of the highest Court should establish the law until modified by statute or by a later decision of the state court, I do not perceive how it would be possible for a Court of the United States to refuse to follow what the State Court decided in that domain. But when the Constitution of the State establishes a Supreme Court it by implication does make that declaration as clearly as if it had said it in express words, so far as it is not interfered with by the superior power of the United States. The Supreme Court of a State does something more than make a scientific inquiry into a fact outside of and independent of it. It says with an authority that no one denies except when a citizen of another State is able to invoke an exceptional jurisdiction that thus the law is and shall be. Whether it be said to make or to declare the law, it deals with the law of the State with equal authority however its function may be described." *Black & White Taxicab & Transfer Co. v. Brown & Yellow Taxicab & Transfer Co.*, 276 U.S. 518, 532, 533-35, (1928) (Holmes, J. dissenting). This dissenting opinion and an article appearing in a law journal discussing the intent of Congress in adopting the Judiciary Act (the article is Warren, Charles, "New Light in the History of the Federal Judiciary Act of 1789," 37 Harvard Law Review 49 (1923)) may have been influential in the *Erie Railroad Co. v. Tompkins* decision.

[92] For additional background information, see Kramer, Mark R., "The Role of Federal Courts in Changing State Law: The Employment at Will Doctrine in Pennsylvania," 133 University of Pennsylvania Law Review 227 (1984).

[93] *Erie Railroad Co. v. Tompkins*, 98 F.2d 49 (2d. Cir. 1938).

[94] Murrill, Brandon J., "The Supreme Court's Overruling of Constitutional Precedent," Congressional Research Service, Updated September 24, 2018: https://fas.org/sgp/crs/misc/R45319.pdf.

As this report indicates, it is common when a precedent is overruled that the court will state that the precedent was incorrectly decided. Sometimes, there will be a series of cases decided after the incorrect precedent that will conflict with the incorrect precedent or will question whether it was correctly decided. The Erie decision is unusual because neither of these approaches is taken. The Supreme Court in Erie seems to view Swift v. Tyson as an effort to achieve uniformity in decisions between state and federal courts. While this is an important principle, Swift v. Tyson did not achieve the desired result.

Instead, the opposite occurred, and the result was that litigants were forum-shopping for which body of law would be most favorable to their position. In short, the consequences of the decision in Swift v. Tyson were not acceptable.

For a well-written discussion of the Erie case and of other cases in which the Supreme Court overruled a prior decision, see Ernst, Morris, *The Great Reversals: Tales of the Supreme Court*, Page 119.

In *The Judge and the Philosopher*, I discuss the Knick v. Township of Scott case. The relevant precedent was the Williamson case and the Supreme Court heard oral argument for the overruling of Williamson when it would be applied to a civil rights claim in a real property case. Williamson, in effect, blocked the property owner in Knick from exercising the right in federal court to exclude other individuals from entering onto her property. The Knick case is a dispute between the owner of a farm which may have an ancient cemetery on the farm and other individuals who apparently want to inspect her farm in an effort to visit the cemetery. It is not clearly stated in the case exactly why they want to enter onto her farm. Maybe, it is historical interest, they may think their relatives are buried on the farm, or it could be curiosity, or even contrariness (a dispute between neighbors). There is very little civil rights law related to owners of cemeteries that may exist on farms having the right to exclude visitors. Similarly, the civil rights of persons who want to search for ancient cemeteries is also an area of the law that is not well developed. It is not clear which of these contesting parties has the strongest claim to a violation of their rights.

What is clear in the *Knick* case, and the reason why I have included it in *The Judge and the Philosopher*, is that the argument was made in the Knick case that the consequences of the Williamson precedent were unacceptable. I use the *Knick* case to illustrate that the argument may be made when arguing in court that a precedent should be overruled when it results in undesirable consequences. In short, the court should make a decision that is not based upon the pre-existing law, but the court should change the law and make a wise decision.

95 *West v. American Telephone & Telegraph Co.*, 311 U.S. 223, 237 (1940).

96 *Ibid.*

97 *Fidelity Union Trust Co. v. Field,* 311 U.S. 169 (1940).

98 *Yoder v. Nu-Enamel Corp.*, 117 F.2d 488 (8th Cir. 1941).

99 *Id.* at 489.

100 Richard A. Posner is associated with the view that judges, as a matter of fact, decide cases based on economic efficiency. Clark, Gordon L., *Judges and the Cities*, Page 46. See also Epstein, Lee, Landes, William M. and Posner, Richard A., *The Behavior of Federal Judges: A Theoretical and Empirical Study of Rational Choice* (this is a book written by a political scientist, an economist and a federal judge describing judicial behavior by referring to a labor economics model).

101 Posner, Richard A., *Law, Pragmatism, and Democracy.*

102 *Ibid.*

103 *Ibid.*

104 Frank, Jerome N., *Law and the Modern Mind*, Page 125. See Green, Michael Stephen, "Legal Realism as Theory of Law,"46 William & Mary Law Review 1915, 1930 (2005).

105 Green argues that a delusional person who sits in the judge's chair and issues an obviously absurd order would not have issued a valid order and the order would be nullity ab initio. The order is obviously void, but it is void not because it is absurd. It is void because it was not issued by an individual with legal authority. Green, Michael Stephen, "Legal Realism as Theory of Law," 46 William & Mary Law Review 1915, 1993 (2005). Richard A. Posner reaches a similar conclusion: "To regard oneself and to be regarded by others, as a good judge requires conformity to the accepted norms of judging. One cannot be regarded as a good judge if one takes bribes, decides cases by flipping coins, falls

asleep in the courtroom, ignores legal doctrine, cannot make up one's mind, bases decisions on the attractiveness or unattractiveness of the litigants or their lawyers, or decides cases on the basis of politics (depending on how that slippery word is defined)." Posner, Richard A., *How Judges Think*, Page 61.

[106] See Commonwealth of Pennsylvania v. County of Bucks, 8 Pa. Commw. 295, 304 A.2d 897 (Pa. Commw. Ct. 1973), <u>cert. denied</u>, 414 U.S. 1130, 94 S. Ct. 869, 38 L.Ed.2d 754 (1974) in which the Commonwealth Court held that the issue was not justiciable. The Commonwealth Court affirmed the decision of the Court of Common Pleas, 22 Bucks Co. L. Rep. 179 (1972). I tried this case, and this decision is discussed in Moskowitz, David H., *Exclusionary Zoning Litigation*, Page 46 (1977) and Reinstein, McFadden, Feder, and Kerper, "A Case of Exclusionary Zoning," 46 Temple Law Quarterly 7 (1972). Justiciability is discussed in more detail in *The Judge and the Rules*.

[107] Shulman, Harry, "The Demise of Swift v. Tyson," Yale Faculty Scholarship Series Paper 4599.
http://digitalcommons.law.yale.edu/fss_pages 4599

Chapter Seven: The Correct, Unjust, Wise Decision

[108] The defects included that the roof eave to wall junctures did not have the appropriate flashing (kick-out flashing), the expansion joints were not adequately sealed, expansion or control joints were lacking, there was a lack of weep screed, above the windows the stucco improperly stopped too tight relative to head flashings located above the windows and doors, all of which led the engineer to recommend that there be a complete stripping off of the exterior façade of the entire house.

[109] *Elderkin v. Gaster*, 447 Pa. 118, 288 A.2d 771 (Pa. 1972).

[110] *Conway v. The Cutler Group, Inc.*, 25 Pa. D. & C. 5th 239 (Bucks County 2012). Judge Waite pointed out that the Conways did not include the Fields in their lawsuit and decided to sue only the builder. Moreover, they did not sue the builder for negligence but based their claim solely on the implied warranty of habitability. They could not sue the builder for breach of contract because they had no contract with the builder. Judge Waite's reading of the pre-existing law is as follows: "Subsequent purchasers obviously do not have a direct contractual relationship with the builder/vendor and the courts have resisted extension of an express warranty given by the builder/vendor to the original purchaser to now cover subsequent purchasers." The Court of Common Pleas did not view this as a gap in the law because it held that, if there is no cause of action, the plaintiff cannot prevail.

[111] *Conway v. Cutler Group, Inc.*, 25 Pa. D. & C.5th 239 (2012).

[112] *Conway v. Cutler Group, Inc.*, 57 A.3d 155 (Pa. Super. 2012).

[113] *Spivack v. Birch Ridge Corp.*, 586 A.2d 402 (Pa. Super. 1990).

[114] *Kaptanovach v. Fox*, 20 Pa. D. & C.4th 316 (C.P. Allegheny 1993).

[115] *Conway v. Cutler Group, Inc.*, 57 A.3d 155 (Pa. Super. 2012).

[116] *Conway v. Cutler Group, Inc.*, 57 A.3d 155 (Pa. Super. 2012).

[117] *Conway v. The Cutler Group*, 626 Pa. 660, 99 A.3d 67 (Pa. 2014).

[118] *Ibid.*

[119] The Supreme Court in the Conway case quoted, with approval, the following reasoning from *Manlin v. Genoe* (City of Philadelphia Police Beneficiary Association), 340 Pa. 320, 17 A.2d 407, 409 (Pa. 1941): "In our judicial system, the power of courts to formulate pronouncements of public policy is sharply restricted; otherwise, they would become judicial legislatures rather than instrumentalities for the interpretation of law. Generally speaking, the Legislature is the body to declare the public policy of a state and to order changes therein. . .

"The right of a court to declare what is or is not in accord with public policy does not extend to specific economic or social problems which are controversial in nature and capable of solution only as the result of a study of various factors and conditions. It is only when a given policy is so obviously for or against the public health, safety, morals or welfare that there is virtually a unanimity of opinion in regard to it that a court may constitute itself the voice of the community in so declaring. . ..

"If, in the domain of economic and social controversies, a court were, under the guise of the application of the doctrine of public policy, in effect to enact provisions which it might consider expedient and desirable, such action would be nothing short of judicial legislation, and each such court would be creating positive laws according to the particular views and idiosyncrasies of its members. Only in the clearest cases, therefore, may a court make an alleged public policy the basis of judicial decision"

[120] Llewellyn, Karl, *The Theory of Rules,* Page 42.
[121] Biddle, Francis, *Mr. Justice Holmes,* Page 49.

Chapter Eight: The Incorrect, Unjust, Wise Decision

[122] *In re Federal Facilities Realty Trust*, 97 F.Supp. 622 (N.D. Ill. 1949).
[123] *Federal Facilities Realty Trust*, 184 F.2d 1 (7th Cir. 1950). Circuit Judge Finnegan quotes from the report of the Special Master in his opinion: "There is not a scintilla of evidence to prove that Mr. Darrow profited in any sum whatsoever through his trading in securities of the trusts . . ." He then quotes from *Remington on Bankruptcy*; Section 2965 as follows "A receiver will not be surcharged . . . where he has exercised due diligence in the selection of a bookkeeper and superintendent even though in fact those employees were incompetent or dishonest." Circuit Judge

Finnegan also quotes from *American Law Institute on Trusts*, Volume 2, Page 1190 similar language. *Perry on Trusts*, Vol. 3, Page 683 also agrees. The appellees (Mosser, et al.) did not cite a single U.S. case providing for a surcharge against a trustee in similar circumstances. Therefore, there was no rule of the pre-existing law allowing for the surcharge and the Court of Appeals made the correct decision.

[124] *Mosser v. Darrow*, 341 U.S. 267, 71 S.Ct. 680 (1951).

[125] *Mosser v. Darrow*, 341 U.S. at 271.

[126] *Mosser v. Darrow*, 341 U.S. at 276 (1951) (Black, J. dissenting).

[127] *Mosser v. Darrow*, 341 U.S. at 271-72.

[128] *Mosser v. Darrow*, 341 U.S. at 273.

[129] *Mosser v. Darrow*, 341 U.S. at 273. The Court also said: "In fairness to the trustee, it is to be noted that there is no hint or proof that he has been corrupt, or that he has any interest, present or future, in the profits he has permitted these employees to make. For all that appears, he was simply misled into thinking these persons indispensable, but he entered into an arrangement that courts cannot sanction unless they are to open the door to practices which should demoralize trusteeships and discredit bankruptcy administration." Ibid.

[130] *Ibid.*

[131] *Id.* at 276 and 684.

[132] There were two cases, *Gratz v. Bollinger*, 539 U.S. 244 (2003) and *Grutten v. Bollinger*, 539 U.S. 306 (2003) and the statement quoted is from the second case. Justice O'Conner's concurring opinion starts on Page 311 and the statement appears on Page 343.

[133] In the second case in the preceding footnote, Justice Thomas' opinion starts on Page 349 and the statement appears on Page 351.

[134] An example appears in an opinion of the Wisconsin Supreme Court [*in Publ v. Milwaukee Auto Ins. Co.*, 8 Wis.2d 343, 354-357, 99 N.W.2d 163, 169-171 (1960]] concerning a claim in a personal

injury case: "The court determined that the evidence presented was insufficient to support the finding that the defendant's conduct caused the personal injury. This was, of course, all that was required for disposition of the case at hand. 'However,' the court added, 'the importance of this problem compels us to point out the present state of the law.' Having thus explained why they were doing so; the court reviewed the shift of the weight of precedents from various states concerning personal injuries and observed the dubious reliability of the Wisconsin precedent." Keeton, Robert E., *Venturing to do Justice*, Page 31.

[135] Id. at 169 contains a list of cases that overruled precedents.

[136] The desirability of narrow rules is recognized by John Dickinson: "What is needed is not arbitrary discretion, but a rule for making exceptions—a rule for breaking a rule, --and of such rules the law is of course full. What is essential is that it should go on generating them as need for them is seen to arise. The law often comes to recognize, as it did not before, a circumstance or set of circumstances as constituting a valid element of difference, removing the facts of a case from the pigeonhole of which they would otherwise properly belong." Dickinson, John, *Administrative Justice and the Supremacy of Law in the United States,* Page *139.*

[137] *See Davies v. Mann*, 1010 M. & W. 546, 152 Eng. Rep. 588 (1842). See also MacIntyre, Malcolm, "The Rationale of Last Clear Chance," 53 Harvard Law Review 1225 (1940) and Jensen, O.C., *The Nature of Legal Argument*, Page 46. The last clear chance rule is discussed in Hart, H.L.A. and Honore, E.M., *Causation in the Law*, Pages 201-07. In the beginning of their analysis, they assert that the last clear chance rule is not a principle, but it is, instead, a rule that allows for the plaintiff to recover if his conduct was less dangerous than that of the defendant. At the end of their discussion, they explain their earlier statement: "Some may think that it is an insult to the man in the street to pretend that the last clear chance rule is an application of *any* common-sense

principle." Id. at 207 (emphasis in original). I am not certain what they are referring to in this statement. My reason for including the last clear chance rule in the text is that it is a good example of how the *ratio decidendi* of the just decision can develop into a broader legal rule.

[138] *Brown v. Board of Education*, 347 U.S. 483 (1954). See Abernethy, George L., *The Idea of Equality*, Page 325 for a discussion of the relief in this case and Berle, Adolf A., *The Three Faces of Power*, Page 12 for the observation that the decision in this case was revolutionary.

[139] *Donoghue v. Stevenson*, (1932) A.C. 562.

[140] Courts must always be conscious of their limitations as courts. See Green, Leon, "The Duty Problem in Negligence Cases," 28 Columbia Law Review 1014, 1034 (1928). There are, no doubt, many places in the law where the possibility of more just decisions exists, but the potentiality of implementing the potential rule that would lead to just decisions creates more problems than the value of the just decision. For example, Lord Mansfield concluded that the application of the pre-existing law was more desirable than the just decision: "The objection, that a contract is immoral or illegal as between plaintiff and defendant, sounds at all times very ill in the mouth of the defendant. It is not for his sake, however, that the objection is ever allowed; but it is found in general principles of policy, which the defendant has the advantage of, contrary to the real justice, as between him and the plaintiff, by accident, if I may say so." *Holmes v. Johnson*, 1 Cowp. 341, 343, 98 Eng. Rep. 1120, 1121 (1778). See Holmes, Oliver Wendell, Jr., *The Common Law*, Page108 and Hart, H.L.A., *The Concept of Law*, Page162. Just as one may tell a young child not to cross the street if he can see any cars coming, not trusting the child's judgment of how fast he can cross the street compared to the speed of a car in the far-off distance, the law may frequently find it expedient to choose rules for the ease of their application rather than attempt distinctions that are too fine for courts of law.

141 Wasserstrom, Richard, *The Judicial Decision*, Page 156. Jonathan Crowe also contends that judicial reasoning has two steps: an interpretive stage where the linguistic meaning of the legal rule is considered and a construction stage where the content of that rule is translated into legal outcomes. Crowe, Jonathan, "The Role of Contextual Meaning in Judicial Interpretation," 41 Federal Law Review 417, 439 (2013).

142 Id. at 136. Wasserstrom's description of the equitable theory is as follows: ". . . [T]he equitable rule of decision prescribes that a decision is justifiable if and only if it produces a maximum of satisfaction and a minimum of dissatisfaction between the litigants." Id. at 167. This is similar to Jerome Frank's view of emphasizing the facts, which I discussed in Section 5.4 and will return to in Chapter Nine. Wasserstrom's equitable theory at other places in his book appears to be similar to the traditional conception of the influence of equity in judicial decisions: ". . . [T]he concept of an equitable procedure of justification rests very largely upon the notion that the peculiar or unique facts of each case ought to be taken into express account and given primary significance in order to do justice in the particular case." Id. at 114.

143 Id. at 171. Wasserstrom's procedure for the justification of judicial decisions is what H. L. A. Hart calls a "two-level" procedure. See Hart, H.L.A., Book Review of Wasserstrom, Richard A., *The Judicial Decision*, 14 Stanford Law Review 917, 919 (1961). Wasserstrom uses a form of utilitarianism which is "restricted" rather than "extensive," so he justifies rules with it rather than particular actions. The judge applies a rule, but the rule also has to be justified—hence, two levels. He combines a formulistic procedure of applying the rule with an equitable procedure which looks only to the result between the parties, with an overlay of utilitarianism.

Chapter Nine: Revisiting the Six Cases

[144] The injustice inherent in retroactive law-application is a central theme in the legal philosophy of Ronald Dworkin. While Hart does not clearly portray the role of justice in the secondary rules, though he seems to flirt with the idea that there is some relationship between law and justice, Dworkin clearly considers justice and many other aspects of morality to be central feature s in his description of the judicial process. Many political philosophers discuss a conflict between law and justice, noting that laws may be just or unjust. Dworkin takes law to be a branch of morality, so that justice and law cannot conflict. Dworkin, Ronald, *Justice for Hedgehogs*, Page 5.

He concludes that there are shared identifiable paradigms of justice. Dworkin, Ronald, *Law's* Empire, Pages74-75. Even though there are paradigm examples of justice, we may disagree about whether a particular action is just or unjust. Dworkin, Ronald, *Justice for Hedgehogs,* Page 160. But, because of our shared understanding, we agree that it would be unjust to convict an innocent man or to tax the hardworking individuals to support those who refuse to work. Id. at 161. We agree to a sufficient extent to develop a concept of justice that reflects our common beliefs. Ibid.

My objection to Dworkin's view of adjudication can be easily demonstrated by considering the Conway case. Dworkin would describe the differences between the three courts that heard the Conway case as a difference in the interpretation of the law. This is misleading because all 3 courts at 3 different levels of the judicial hierarchy were in agreement about the legal rule established in the Elderkin case. The difference between the courts was based on whether the court should change the rule (the implied warranty of habitability) or not change the rule. There was complete agreement about what the law is, and, in that sense, all the judges involved in the case were operating in accordance with Hart's rule of recognition which led them all to the same conclusion about what the correct decision would be. The issue in the Conway case, at all 3 levels of the judicial hierarchy, was not "what is the law," but whether the law should be modified.

Given that the law was determinate in the Conway case, Hart's description of the judicial process works for the trial court and the Supreme Court. It does not accurately portray the approach of the Superior Court, the intermediate appellate court, which wanted to expand the legal rule to include second purchasers (the legal rule in the Elderkin case applied only to the initial purchaser). The Superior Court wanted to decide in favor of the Conways in order to make what I would call a just decision and one could view it as also a wise decision (the judges in the Superior Court thought it would be a wise decision, but I am not sure that I agree with their conclusion, and, in fact, I think that the correct decision was the more desirable decision).

In addition, and even more important, Dworkin's various theories distort my concept of the correct decision. "The law is _____" is necessarily a statement with a particular geographical location in mind at a particular point in time. If you do not accept the separation theory and the difference between "is" and "ought," you lose the temporal/special context of the statement and the statement becomes meaningless. I explain this last point in *The Judge and the Philosopher.*

For example, Swift v. Tyson was the law for almost 100 years in every federal court jurisdiction in the United States. The legal rule changed when Erie Railroad Co. v. Tompkins was decided. If you argue that the Erie Doctrine was the law before the Erie case was decided, when in the almost 100 years after the decision in the Swift case did the law change? If you asked the question of "what is the law?" in 1900, 1910, 1920, or 1930, would your answer presuppose that the Erie Doctrine was the law? Dworkin's "law as integrity" cannot accurately portray the changes in the legal rules or the actuality of what the law is before the change in the law occurs. Consequently, Dworkin's theory does not accurately portray the correct decision and the changes in the law when the correct decision is not made.

But my presentation of creative positivism may not be as different from Dworkin's theory as I have suggested. Dworkin makes the following statement: "…[I]n very rare cases judges may have a moral obligation to ignore the law when it is very unjust or perhaps when it is very unwise …". Dworkin, Ronald, *Justice in Robes*, Page18. To be fair to Dworkin, this is just an isolated statement and he hedges this view by using the terms "very rare," "perhaps," and "very unwise." If you ignore those terms ("very" two times and "perhaps"), it sounds like Dworkin could accept creative positivism.

[145] Llewellyn, Karl, *The Theory of Rules,* Page147. In *Newland v. Sebelius*, 881 F.Supp.2d 1287 (D. Colo. 2012), aff'd, 542 F.App'x 706 (10th Cir. 2013), Judge John I. Kane restricts his ruling in the case to the litigants in the case. The District Court did not enjoin enforcement of the preventive care coverage mandate against any other party.

[146] Justice Brandeis in the Erie case accepted the definition of the law in Swift v. Tyson and added to that definition the legal rules established in authoritative precedents. See Chapter Six where these two cases are discussed.

Chapter Ten: Creative Positivism

[147] W.J. Auden, in a poem called" Law, Like Love" includes the following lines:

>"Law, says the judge, as he looks down his nose,
>   Speaking clearly and most severely,
>   Law is as I've told you before.

Law is as you know I suppose,

Law is but let me explain it once more,

Law is The Law."

[148] Baum, Lawrence, *Judges and Their Audiences,* Page 113 makes this observation: "Judges are socialized in their [legal] norms, and lawyers and other judges are important audiences. These judges want to see themselves as people who follow their duties under the law, and they want others to see them in the same way."

[149] Baum, Lawrence, *Judges and Their Audiences*, Page 112.

[150] Auerbach, Carl A., Garrison, Lloyd K., Hurst, Willard and Morrison Samuel., *The Legal Process,* Page 183.

[151] For a discussion of the many factors involved in judges deciding cases, including rationalization, see Love, Mary C., *Human Conduct and the Law*, Page 6. Isaiah Berlin declares that "Every judgment is relative, every evaluation subjective, made what and as it is by the interplay of the factors of its own time and place, individual or collective." Berlin, Isaiah, *Historical Inevitability*, Page 59.

[152] Gardner, John, "The Legality of Law," 17 Ratio Juris 168, 174 (2004). See also Young, Ernest A., "A General Defense of <u>Erie Railroad Co. v. Tompkins</u>," 10 Journal of Law, Economics and Policy 17, 93 (2013): "Adjudication of disputes under preexisting law, whether statutory or constitutional, is distinct from lawmaking, and the judiciary's power to do one is not necessarily coextensive even with its *own* power to do the other." This is followed by Footnote 44 in which after cases are cited, he mentions: "As discussed earlier, none of this is to deny that every adjudication may involve a sort of Heisenbergian element of lawmaking."

[153] See Gardner, John, "Legal Positivism: 5 and ½ Myths," 46 American Journal of Jurisprudence 199, 201 (2002) where he suggests that "soft" or "inclusive" positivists assert that norms may be legally valid in virtue of their merits if there are legal norms which validate them. In other words, a standard of merit is part of the legal system. "Hard" or "exclusive" positivists would

deny this and would contend that there are no legal norms that would invalidate norms based upon merit.

154 R (on the application of Miller, Appellant) v. The Prime Minister (Respondent) v. Advocate General for Scotland (Appellant): https://www.telegraph.co.uk/politics/2019/09/24/supreme-court-ruling-lady-hales-prorogation-statement-full/

Chapter Eleven: Conclusion

155 *See Gohmert v. Pence*, 2021 U.S. Dist. LEXIS 3 (decided on January 1, 2021 by Judge Jeremy Kernodle in the Eastern District Court of Texas), which was affirmed by the Court of Appeals on January 2, 2021, 2021 U.S. Appl LEXIS 9 (5th Circuit Court of Appeals) by Per Curium Order. It was decided by a three-judge panel and the opinion was written for the court and not by a particular named judge. The opinion is not a published opinion and has no status as a precedent.

156 *Ibid.*

Appendix C

157 Hamilton, Peter J., "The Civil Law and the Common Law," 36 Harvard Law Review 180, 192 (1991).

These citations are all available at www.creativepositivist.com

Index

A

G

H

I

DAVID H. MOSKOWITZ

Dave practiced law for approximately 50 years (now retired) and has been involved in entrepreneurial ventures of different types during that same period and at the present time. He spends his days working on his real estate projects or his biopharma projects, and writing books.

He is married to Marian (they have celebrated their 37th anniversary) and they have raised five children and have five grandchildren. Marian is the Chairlady of the Chester County Commissioners, and a board member of multiple non-profit institutions. They live in Malvern, Chester County, Pennsylvania.

You can contact the author via his website
www.thecreativepositivist.com

www.ingramcontent.com/pod-product-compliance
Lightning Source LLC
Chambersburg PA
CBHW041208220326
41597CB00030BA/5107